Cranbrook

THE CAMPUS GUIDE

Cranbrook

Kathryn Bishop Eckert
Photographs by Balthazar Korab
Foreword by Robert M. Gavin, Jr.

Princeton Architectural Press
NEW YORK | *2001*

This book has been made possible through the generous support
of the Graham Foundation for Advanced Studies in the Fine Arts.

Princeton Architectural Press
37 East 7th Street
New York, NY 10003
212.995.9620

For a free catalog of books published by Princeton Architectural Press,
call toll free 1.800.722.6657 or visit our web site at www.papress.com.

05 04 03 02 01 5 4 3 2 1 FIRST EDITION
Printed in China

Editing: Jan Cigliano
Series concept: Dennis Looney
Copyediting: Heather Ewing
Design: Sara E. Stemen
Layout: Mary-Neal Meador
Maps: Jane Garvie
Special thanks to Ann Alter, Amanda Atkins, Nicola Bednarek, Eugenia Bell,
Caroline Green, Beth Harrison, Mia Ihara, Clare Jacobson, Mark Lamster, Anne Nitschke,
Lottchen Shivers, Jennifer Thompson, and Deb Wood of Princeton Architectural Press
—Kevin C. Lippert, *publisher*

Library of Congress Cataloguing-in-Publication Data
Eckert, Kathryn Bishop (1935–)
The campus guide : Cranbrook / Kathryn Bishop Eckert — 1st ed.
p. cm.
Includes bibliographical references and index.
ISBN 1-56898-257-7 (pbk. : alk. paper)
1. Cranbrook—Guidebooks. 2. Cranbrook—Buildings—Guidebooks.
3. Cranbrook—Buildings—History I. Title.
LD7501.B6083E35 2001
711'.57'0977438—dc21 00-046955
CIP

How to use this book vi

Foreword by Robert M. Gavin, Jr. vii

Introduction 1

Woodward Avenue Entrance: Gateway to the Campus 11

Walk 1 **Homestead Properties** 16

Walk 2 **Brookside Lower School** 38

Walk 3 **Christ Church Cranbrook** 52

Walk 4 **Cranbrook Campus of Cranbrook Kingswood School** 68

Walk 5 **Cranbrook Academy of Art and Museum** 94

Walk 6 **Kingswood Campus** 122

Walk 7 **Cranbrook Institute of Science** 138

Walk 8 **Bloomfield HIlls, Birmingham, Warren, and Fenton** 152

Walk 9 **Detroit** 162

Bibliography 174

Checklist of Significant Works of Art 181

Acknowledgments 184

Index 185

How to use this book

This guide is intended for visitors, alumni, and students who wish to have an insider's look at the most historic and interesting buildings on campus—from the Cranbrook Academy of Art by Eliel Saarinen, to Bertram Goodhue's Christ Church Cranbrook, to Williams Natatorium by Tod Williams and Billie Tsien, and the Cranbrook Institute of Science, recently renovated and expanded by Steven Holl.

The book is divided into nine Walks, arranged geographically and chronologically by area within Cranbrook Educational Community and Christ Church Cranbrook. Each Walk, or section, is introduced by an historical overview, followed by a list of buildings illustrated on a three-dimensional map, with entries of historical and architectural information and photographs. The last two Walks are conceived as driving tours. They cover buildings in Bloomfield Hills, Birmingham, Warren, and Fenton (Walk Eight) and in Detroit (Walk Nine).

Cranbrook is a private school and many buildings on campus are homes to students, faculty and their families, and staff members—day and night. Please do not enter classrooms or residential buildings.

Cranbrook buildings are closed to the public, except for those mentioned below.
Grounds open: 6AM–6PM daily, year-round.
Cranbrook Art Museum: 10AM–5PM Tuesday–Sunday, with extended hours
    Thursday until 8PM, September–May; extended hours Friday until
    10PM, June–August.
Admission: $5 adults; $3 seniors 65+ and full-time students.
Cranbrook Institute of Science: 10AM–5PM daily, with extended hours Friday
    and Saturday until 10PM Memorial Day–Labor Day.
Admission: $7 adults; $4 seniors 65+ and children 3–17. Planetarium and laser
    shows an additional fee.
Saarinen House: various times, May–October.
Cranbrook House open for guided tours: Thursday 11AM and 1:15PM, Sunday
    1:30PM and 3PM, mid-June–late September.
Admission, including the gardens: $10 adults; $8 seniors.
Cranbrook Gardens open for self-guided tours: May–Labor Day, daily
    10AM–5PM; Sunday 11AM–5PM; after Labor Day, daily 11AM–3PM;
    October, weekends only 11AM–3PM.
Admission: $5 adults; $4 seniors and students.
Christ Church Cranbrook: for information and to make a tour reservation
    248.644.5210.

Further Information from:
    Cranbrook Public Relations
    39221 North Woodward Avenue
    Bloomfield Hills, MI 48303-0801
    1-877-GO-CRANBrook

Nearly one hundred years after Cranbrook's founding in 1904, our campus is undergoing an architectural renaissance not experienced since its earliest days. In 1925 George and Ellen Booth brought Finnish-American architect Eliel Saarinen to the campus. For the next two decades, they collaborated with Saarinen to create an educational community like no other—a place where art, architecture, science, and nature would co-exist in harmony.

The Booths and Saarinen envisioned a campus built with the finest materials and designed to be working spaces, yet spaces that inspired awe and an earnestness to seek further knowledge. Saarinen's first buildings, Cranbrook School for Boys, reflected George Booth's desire for an English-style boarding school. But Saarinen melded that architectural approach with a soaring tower, sunken football field, arches, and sweeping vistas.

His work through the years would integrate his vision of twentieth-century modernism with the Arts and Crafts and Art Deco movements. The Cranbrook Art Museum's peristyle appears simple in form but makes a bold and lasting impression. The Institute of Science integrated natural materials and smooth lines, perfectly suiting its purpose as a natural history museum. Saarinen's masterpiece, Kingswood, is thoroughly modern in design, yet its details—the stair-stepped columns, expansive copper roof, intricately designed geometric windows, interior furnishings, tiling, and textiles—make it a true work of art. And despite its enormous footprint and scale, Kingswood appears in context with the surrounding wooded areas and lake.

These are Cranbrook's architectural treasures. They are the built legacy that we hand down from generation to generation, making the responsibility for properly and thoughtfully caring for these buildings even more awesome. As decades turned into a half century and now nearly a century, we recently have begun meticulously restoring everything from Pewabic tile floors to intricately carved wooden doors. We are upgrading the more mundane systems such as plumbing and electrical lines. We are finding ways to be more energy efficient and we are nurturing the land—our forests, waterways, and fields.

The idea of adding new buildings to a campus that has become a National Historic Landmark—known internationally for its extraordinary architecture—is nothing short of daunting. But Cranbrook could not continue the vision of its founders without continuing to look to the future. As George Booth said, "We had but one purpose, and that was to do something here at Cranbrook that was going to serve this state first and the world next. . . . But the question is, what will we do tomorrow? We are not through."

We took this charge seriously, knowing that, like Saarinen, the architects adding to this campus would make lasting impressions that affected generations after. We chose Peter Rose, whose credits include an American Institute of Architects national honor award, to add to Brookside Lower School—expanding the elementary classrooms, designing striking science and music spaces, and creating early childhood classrooms built to match the scale of tiny hands. His design reflects the "nook and cranny" quality of the original school, taking into account the children using the building and giving it an appropriate character and rhythm.

Internationally known architect Steven Holl approached the Institute of Science expansion and renovation with the same search for form that Saarinen began. Holl's design allows for an unending loop through the building and exemplifies the scientific principle that opposites attract. The long, narrow halls in his building connect with the original minimally, seemingly because of a magnetic friction between the two structures. The connection, however, creates an exquisite, hidden courtyard, and Holl's choice of colored cement block as the major building material complements Saarinen's natural scheme.

Architectural duo Tod Williams and Billie Tsien, among *Newsweek's* list of 100 people to watch in the new millennium, brought a poetic aesthetic to their design of Cranbrook's natatorium. A 1961 Cranbrook graduate, Tod Williams knew Saarinen's work well and drew on Saarinen's belief that buildings must be set in context. Williams has said that the design "interweaves the natatorium with Cranbrook's academic buildings and landscape, combining the intellectual and physical worlds, art and architecture, the natural and built environment, rather than setting the building in isolation." Combining richly colored, sand-cast and glazed bricks, the building is natural and overwhelmingly beautiful. Williams and Tsien will continue their dialogue with Cranbrook's architecture as the team responsible for future phases of athletic buildings on campus.

As this book goes to press, we will break ground on new studios for the academy of art. Pritzker prize-winning architect Rafael Moneo's building will seamlessly connect with Saarinen's art museum. A dramatic atrium and free-standing stairway will give way to new gallery spaces, which in turn give way to working artist studios and then to more austere and functional machinery spaces for kilns and metalsmithing shops. The building's design reflects those changing uses, subtly transforming from a museum style to a straight-lined industrial form.

Each building reflects the spirit of collaboration and connection originally envisioned by the Booths and Saarinen. Yet each building also carefully represents a new inquiry and a different time in our history.

I hope that you will come see our campus. Stand under the art museum's peristyle and look across Carl Milles's sculptures. Walk the gardens. Tour Eliel Saarinen's restored home. Stop beside our mastodon and view the expansive institute exhibition halls. While here, you likely will see some of our 1,500 students. Please remember that Cranbrook functions in the way originally intended, as a vital, active place for students, artists, and scientists. Let them continue their work.

Robert M. Gavin, Jr.
President

Introduction

Cranbrook lies twenty miles northwest of Detroit in Bloomfield Hills. Here, in Oakland County, the Huron and Erie glacial lobes collided, creating rolling hills and depositing granite boulders. The 315-acre campus is covered with woods, meadows, and gardens; and four branches of the River Rouge and its tributaries flow through. Surrounding the campus are large suburban houses and country estates built by wealthy Detroiters. The vernacular design of the Cranbrook architecture, its craftsman detail, sculpture, art, and landscaping distinctively impart the interests of the founders to the campus. Together with the granite fieldstone boulders that wall the homestead property (Cranbrook House and Gardens) and with the Gothic church (Christ Church Cranbrook), these buildings identify the campus with Oakland County in southeast Lower Michigan and with George Gough Booth, Detroit newspaper publisher, and his wife Ellen (Nellie) Warren Scripps Booth. Their lives were shaped by the English Arts and Crafts Movement— that is, the integration of art and religion; an emphasis on the vernacular; and a utilization of arts and crafts as part of daily life and work, rather than as separate professionalized endeavors.[1] Booth himself was a skilled metal worker and artisan printer. His own Cranbrook Press was modeled after William Morris's Kelmscott Press.

In 1906 Booth organized the Detroit Society of Arts and Crafts and served as its first president. The Detroit Society of Arts and Crafts modeled itself after the Boston Society of Arts and Crafts, in turn inspired by the English Arts and Crafts Movement. In England the Arts and Crafts Movement sought simplicity, beauty, and craftsmanship through the involvement of artists in all aspects of decorative and applied arts. The purpose of the Detroit society was "to encourage good and beautiful work as applied to useful service."[2] Although part of an international movement, the Detroit architects and designers who became members of the society—including Albert Kahn and Mary Chase Perry Stratton—considered the monotonous standardization of industrial methods detrimental to society and sought to remedy this through design.

Cranbrook's 315 acres comprise seven distinct architecturally significant areas, woven together by landscape and unparalleled campus furnishings. Brookside School is sited on a branch of the River Rouge at the northeast corner of Lone Pine and Cranbrook Roads. Cranbrook School, grouped around courtyards, is one-half mile west of Cranbrook Road on the north side of Lone Pine Road. North of Cranbrook School on the east side of Vaughan Road in the former Vaughan School is the boys' middle school. Kingswood School, made up of joined quadrangles and low wings, overlooks Kingswood Lake one mile north of Brookside School on Cranbrook Road. Cranbrook Academy of Art and Museum, with its courts and ells facing away from the entrances and overlooking a wide expanse of rolling meadow, is north of Lone Pine Road along Academy Way. Cranbrook Institute of Science is in a wooded area west of Kingswood and south of the Woodward entrance road. From one of the two highest points on the campus, Cranbrook House and Gardens (the George Gough and Ellen Warren Scripps Booth House) and the homestead properties oppose the art museum and library of the art academy. Each area is distinct. Separate but historically related to Cranbrook stands Christ Church Cranbrook on a ridge at the southwest corner of the intersection of Lone Pine and Cranbrook Roads. All but the last two Walks of this guide are organized as tours; each Walk begins with an historical overview that discusses the origins and inspiration of the particular institution.

Cranbrook was built in the twentieth century through the generosity of George Gough and Ellen Warren Scripps Booth. The Booths employed many architects, artists, and craftsmen to help them transform their country estate into one of the most distinctive educational complexes in the world. Eliel Saarinen, esteemed Finnish-American architect, designed many of the campus's plans and buildings between 1925 and 1942. But Booth articulated the vision for the educational complex, assembled advisors to help shape it, selected architects to give it form, and provided—together with his wife Ellen Booth—the financial means to execute it. He also collaborated with the architects and artists to furnish it with unequaled artistic character.[3]

George Gough Booth House, Detroit; Mason and Rice, architects, 1889; photograph 1900–05, Detroit Publishing Company; Library of Congress

George Gough Booth (1864–1949), Cranbrook Archives

Ellen Warren Scripps Booth (1863–1948), Cranbrook Archives

In 1904 the Booths purchased the Samuel Alexander Farm, comprising about 175 acres in Bloomfield Township. They named it Cranbrook for the English birthplace and ancestral home of Booth's father in Kent. Although the land had many natural features that would lend themselves to transformation into a beautiful summer and recreational country estate, the farm was rundown. The orchards and vineyard had declined, and the fields yielded only meager crops of wheat, corn, rye, and hay. The millpond had been dry ever since the dam had washed out ten years earlier, and the millrace and brook were filled with silt. The Booths set out to acquire and exchange additional land, so that eventually they held over 300 acres in all, on which stood clusters of farm buildings and the remains of a grist mill.

To reclaim the land, first as a self-supporting working farm with an aesthetic vision and later as an educational campus, the Booths employed two professionals intermittently from 1910 until 1923: H. J. Corfield, an English-born horticulturist and superintendent of Scripps Park in Detroit, the site of the Booth's first house; and Ossian Cole Simonds, a teacher of landscape design at the University of Michigan and a proponent of the Midwestern landscape. Under the direction of the Booths, Corfield and a group of Italian American laborers—including Michael (Mike) Vettraino, who would garden for fifty years at Cranbrook—removed trees and underbrush, dammed the River Rouge to create Kingswood Lake, constructed a waterworks cascade on the site of a grist mill, enlarged the millrace, graded the old mill road, constructed a new bridge over the race upstream from the cascade, created several miles of perfectly graded driveways, made lawn, and carried out extensive planting plans.[4] Simonds suggested much of the early landscape scheme, which to a certain extent overlaid forest planting on the farm land.

Cranbrook Farm #2, Marcus R. Burrowes, architect, 1911; photograph circa 1917, Cranbrook Archives

Cranbrook Boys School, Eliel Saarinen, architect, 1926; Cranbrook Archives

At the outset, in 1904, the Booths rehabilitated Alexander's upright-and-wing farmhouse, adding a porch that swept across the front. The house stood on the west side of Cranbrook Road across from the entrance to the present Thornlea House. They used the house as a summer home for themselves, as well as a winter home for George Booth's parents, Henry Wood and Clara Louise Irene Gagnier Booth. Cranbrook House, the Booth's large English Arts and Crafts-style house designed by Albert Kahn, went up in 1907 to 1908. Kahn and Marcus R. Burrowes, also a Detroit architect, prepared plans for farm structures built at the site of Kingswood and Cranbrook Schools and service buildings at Cranbrook House. The farm buildings at Cranbrook would serve as the footprint of the boys' school.

The first community-gathering place, the Meeting House, was built in 1918 to the vernacular English cottage designs of Booth and his son, Henry Scripps Booth. In the following years the Meeting House was added to and expanded to serve as Brookside School. Between 1925 and 1928 Christ Church Cranbrook was constructed to the Gothic plans of Oscar H. Murray of Bertram G. Goodhue and Associates.

In 1925 Saarinen, then visiting professor of architecture at the University of Michigan in Ann Arbor, accepted Booth's invitation to develop a fanciful plan for an academy of art at Cranbrook—one that would comprise instruction in a wide range of artistic disciplines, including fine and applied arts, architecture, the performing arts, and even horticulture. Booth, however, rejected the plan as too grandiose, and it was never carried out.

Saarinen had come to Chicago with his family a few years earlier to see for himself the American Midwest, having won second prize in the Chicago Tribune Tower competition of 1922, with an entry that Louis Sullivan had called a "splendid interpretation of the spirit of the American people."[5]

Saarinen's first completed work at Cranbrook, the Cranbrook School for Boys of 1926–1928, continued the retrospective themes that Kahn, Burrowes, Murray, and Booth had explored in earlier Cranbrook buildings. Beginning with the academy structures of the late 1920s, however, Saarinen utilized more contemporary forms. At Kingswood he followed a prairie school design and used courtyards and terraces. The science institute and the art academy's art library and museum show a modern classical appearance with the landscape in tiered terraces with pools. All were ornamented with sculpture.

Cranbrook Boys School dining hall, Eliel Saarinen, architect, 1928–29; photograph 1935, Cranbrook Archives

In 1927 Booth established the Cranbrook Foundation to endow and support the institutional development of Cranbrook. The completion of undertakings in connection with existing institutions, the development of the Cranbrook Academy of Art and School of Arts and Crafts, and the construction of Kingswood fell to the trustees of the foundation. At the time of the foundation's creation, the endowment of the five institutions and the church was $12 million. The trustees were Gustavus D. Pope, neighbor and associate of Booth in the Detroit Society of Arts and Crafts, manufacturer, president of the American Red Cross, and vice president of the Detroit Community Fund; Henry Schoolcraft Hulbert, friend and judge of probate in Wayne County; Samuel Simpson Marquis, first rector of Christ Church Cranbrook; and three of Booth's sons—Warren Scripps Booth, treasurer of the *Detroit News;* James Scripps Booth, automotive engineer and artist; and Henry Scripps Booth, architect.

Kingswood Girls School entrance gates, Eliel Saarinen, architect, 1930–31; George W. Hance, photographer, Cranbrook Archives

Kingswood Girls School dining hall, Eliel Saarinen, architect, 1930–31; George W. Hance, photographer, Cranbrook Archives

Booth thought that each of the Cranbrook institutions needed time to grow independently of the others to gain its own experience. Each was, therefore, established as an autonomous entity, but it was Booth's hope that the institutions would work in concert.

By the early 1970s the various Cranbrook boards of trustees concluded that it would be in the best fiscal interests of all the Cranbrook institutions to combine. In 1973 the Cranbrook Foundation and five of the original six Cranbrook institutions agreed to reorganize as Cranbrook Educational Community. Christ Church Cranbrook, bowing to church canon, did not participate in the reorganization. Under the new trust, the three Cranbrook Schools were organized as the Cranbrook Schools division,

Kingswood Girls School; photograph 1938, Cranbrook Archives

to complement the Cranbrook Academy of Art division, and the Cranbrook Institute of Science division. The Cranbrook Foundation ceased to exist.

Today Cranbrook Schools comprise Cranbrook Kingswood Upper School, formed in 1984, when Cranbrook School for Boys and Kingswood School for Girls merged; Brookside Lower School for pre-kindergarten to grade five; and Cranbrook Kingswood Middle School with gender-separate programs for grades six to eight. Cranbrook Schools are independent, day and boarding, college preparatory schools that seek to prepare young men and women from diverse backgrounds to develop intellectually, morally, and physically; to move into higher education with competence and confidence; and to appreciate the arts. The schools strive to instill in students a strong sense of social responsibility and the ability to communicate and contribute in an increasingly global community.

Cranbrook Academy of Art is an internationally renowned center for the arts and culture. One hundred fifty graduate students study for two years with faculty comprising ten artists-in-residence. The academy offers the master of architecture degree and the master of fine arts degree in ceramics, two-and three-dimensional design, fiber, metalsmithing, painting, photography, printmaking, and sculpture. Cranbrook Art Museum is a forum for contemporary art, crafts, architecture, and design, dedicated to engaging and educating diverse regional, national, and international audiences.

Cranbrook Institute of Science is a natural history and science museum that fosters in its audience a passion for understanding the world around them and for life-long love of learning. Through its broadly based educational programs, its permanent and changing exhibits, and its collections and research, the institute strives to develop a science-literate public able to cope with today's knowledge-based society.

Cranbrook House and Gardens interprets the lives of Cranbrook's founders, George and Ellen Booth, and is used for both public and private purposes. Receptions, conferences, and tours take place in the first floor of Cranbrook House and the gardens. Its works of art, first floor furnishings, and gardens speak of the Booth family's gracious lifestyle. Administrative offices are located in the upper floors of the house.

In the 1970s Booth Newspapers, Inc., a chain of Michigan papers, was sold to the Newhouse group. And in 1986, Cranbrook received $45 million dollars from the proceeds of the sale of its stock in The Evening News Association, the parent company of *The Detroit News* and other media organizations, to the Gannett Company, Inc. This pool of funds, together with financial strategies like issuing bonds, seeking gifts, and investing in the market, has enabled Cranbrook to support a massive restoration and construction effort leading up to its centennial in 2004.

Planning for a dramatic building campaign took place in the mid-1980s. The trustees, governors, administrators, faculty, and staff of Cranbrook Educational Community, with the assistance of their consultants Hellmuth, Obata & Kassabaum, Touche Ross, and the Taft Group, collaborated in preparing *The Cranbrook Vision: A Community Perspective*. Approved in 1986, this master plan was intended to set the course for the people, programs, and places of the community in the future. The plan recommended opening a northern access to the campus off Woodward Avenue; repairing and restoring buildings, art, and landscaping to correct deferred maintenance; adding classroom, laboratory, and music studio space at Brookside School; constructing an athletic facility with a swimming pool; rehabilitating and expanding the institute of science; and constructing new studios for the art academy.

To address the architectural aspects of *The Cranbrook Vision: A Community Perspective* then president Lillian Bauder convened the Cranbrook Architectural Advisory Council, comprising Keith Kleckner, an official at Oakland University and a trustee of Cranbrook Educational Community; George Herbst, vice president of finance and administration for Cranbrook Educational Community; Dan Hoffman, architect-in-residence at Cranbrook Academy of Art; Jon Hlafter, university architect at Princeton University; and herself. The council was responsible for recommending the selection of architects for the new projects and reviewing the physical development of Cranbrook as defined by the master plan.

The result is an extraordinary group of new buildings and additions to existing buildings: the New Wing of Brookside Lower School by Peter Rose, the Williams Natatorium by Tod Williams and Billie Tsien, and the new addition and renovation to the Cranbrook Institute of Science by Steven Holl. Construction of the studios addition at the Cranbrook Academy of Art by Rafael Moneo is underway in 2000.

The new construction that Cranbrook has undertaken is compatible with both the historic character of each complex and of the campus as a whole. Each new project has been designed to be as unobtrusive as possible and to assure the preservation of the character-defining features of the property and environment.

In addition, architects, designers, and fabricators working under the direction of former academy architect Dan Hoffman, have created bridges, furniture, light standards, and other structures and objects to enhance interior spaces and the grounds.

On June 29, 1989, the U. S. Secretary of the Interior listed Cranbrook a National Historic Landmark. Cranbrook Educational Community takes pride in this highest level of historical designation and conscientiously serves as steward of its heritage.

Under the leadership of Robert M. Gavin, Jr., president of Cranbrook Educational Community, historic preservation of the campus is a primary focus and forms a critical component of Cranbrook's master plan. Many projects have been completed and others are in the planning stage. Ambitious landscape and horticulture preservation plans are under preparation with the realization that hydrology problems must be dealt with before bricks and mortar restoration is fully undertaken. Much restoration work has been undertaken on buildings and sculpture. Full, accurate museum-quality restoration has been completed at Saarinen House; the Greek Theatre; the Triton Pools, sculptures, and landscape; and the millrace and waterwheel. At Cranbrook House and Gardens, Mr. Booth's office and the entry court have been restored. At Kingswood School ceramic tiles glazed green to replicate the original tiles fired at Pewabic Pottery have been laid in the floor of the Green Lobby, and underway is the in-kind replacement of the distinctive copper roof. The approximately six thousand original windows on campus are being repaired in a shop at Cranbrook. Brickwork is undergoing tuckpointing. Many bronze sculptures have been restored, and an annual maintenance plan is in place for all outdoor sculpture. Pavers and a snow-melt system have been installed in the automobile court at 520 Lone Pine Road. This work represents a vision of the future walkways of the Cranbrook School Quadrangle, when additional restoration is undertaken.

Paul Goldberger wrote, "In some ways, Eliel Saarinen's campus is itself Cranbrook's greatest legacy, a collection of buildings that are only now achieving the recognition they deserve as comprising one of the greatest campuses ever created in the world."[6] Cranbrook boasts one of the most outstanding groups of educational structures in the world. Fully aware of both its preservationist and its visionary roles, Cranbrook shares this enchanting place with the world.

1.   Diane Balmori, "Cranbrook: The Invisible Landscape," *Journal of the Society of Architectural Historians* 53, no. 1 (March 1994).

2.   Joy Hakanson Colby, *Art and a City: A History of the Detroit Society of Arts and Crafts* (Detroit, Wayne State University Press, 1956): 4.

3.   From this perspective, Mark Coir, Cranbrook archivist, stresses that "George Gough Booth can be viewed as the primary agent of Cranbrook's programmatic and physical development, as well as a major influence in its architectural development." Mark Coir, *George Bough Booth and the Planning of Cranbrook*, Detroit, Wayne State University, April 1992. Copy in Cranbrook Archives.

4.   This work is summarized in a letter of recommendation for Corfield. George Gough Booth to Whom it May Concern, April 20, 1908, George Gough Booth Papers, Cranbrook Archives.

5.   Louis Sullivan, "The Chicago Tribune Competition," *Architectural Record* 53 (February 1923): 152–153.

6.   Paul Goldberger, "The Cranbrook Vision," *New York Times Magazine* Section 6 (April 8, 1984): 56.

Woodward Avenue Entrance:
Gateway to the Campus

As Cranbrook Educational Community consciously embraced its more
public role first studied in the 1950s under Henry Scripps Booth and more
seriously in the 1980s, it recognized the need to create a common public
access. This need was heightened, in part, by the consequences of the land-
locked siting of the Cranbrook Institute of Science and the traffic that the
institute had generated.

In the fall of 1985 Cranbrook purchased property at the corner of
the intersection of Woodward Avenue (Michigan 1) and Cranbrook Road.
Johnson, Johnson & Roy of Ann Arbor was hired to prepare a site analysis
and an environmental assessment and to develop road alignment alternatives
for an entrance off Woodward Avenue, the historic road that links Detroit to
northern communities.

Like entrances to shopping malls, corporate headquarters, and
community colleges, the Woodward Avenue entrance to Cranbrook is for
automobiles. As Cranbrook developed, each area—with the exception of the
Cranbrook Institute of Science—had a separate and distinct entrance from
Cranbrook, Lone Pine, to Vaughan Road. The entrances accommodated
the transportation mode of the time. In the 1900s the main entrance to
Cranbrook House from Lone Pine Road anticipated arrival by horse and

Woodward Avenue Entrance

carriage or by automobile. In the 1920s the main entrance gate to Cranbrook
School from Lone Pine Road admitted pedestrians into the large academic
quadrangle. In the 1930s the Kingswood entrance was designed for the automobile; the road led through gates to an oval drive with drop-off points
along the northern side of the building. A ceremonial, but seldom used,
entrance for pedestrians fabricated in 1941 leads through majestic gates
across grass to the academy's library and art museum. Cranbrook Institute of
Science, the community's most public building, was reached by way of
Academy and Institute Ways. Each area had its own parking lot. During the
twentieth century as automobile travel increased, parking lots were added
near the areas. People traveling from their cars to their destinations on campus trod paths, creating a vernacular system of pathways.

Northern access to the Cranbrook campus afforded by the
vehicular entrance created at Woodward Avenue offers several distinct
advantages. First, it leaves areas of historical significance on the Cranbrook
campus undisturbed. Second, it ensures the preservation of open space
among Cranbrook House and Gardens, Cranbrook Institute of Science, and
Cranbrook Academy of Art and Museum. Pedestrian paths link these areas
of great natural beauty and cultivated landscape. Third, it gives easy public
access to the popular Cranbrook Institute of Science, which has the greatest
public attendance on campus. Finally, northern access to the campus from
Woodward Avenue increases the security of the schools by sequestering them
somewhat from the more public areas. At the same time, it opens the pastoral
Cranbrook campus to a wider state, national, and international public.

The Gateway to the Campus at 39221 Woodward Avenue was
designed by Dan Hoffman, Ted Gallante, and Juhani Pallasmaa in
1994–1995. Cranbrook, having decided to create an entrance to the campus
from Woodward Avenue, one of Michigan's busiest roads, held a limited
design competition for six select architects. Needed was an extraordinary
structure to inform automobile travelers at medium-to-high speed along
Woodward Avenue about the essence of Cranbrook. The architects were
charged with creating an appropriate contemporary reading of the
Cranbrook campus through an entrance feature. The competition began in
November 1991 and ended in February 1992. Although jurors favored a proposal by Rudolfo Machado and Jorge Silvetti, no clear-cut winner emerged.
Instead, Cranbrook officials chose to proceed with a design by Dan
Hoffman, Cranbrook's architect-in-residence and head of the Cranbrook
Academy of Art's Architecture Department, created in consultation with
Ted Gallante and Juhani Pallasmaa, one of Finland's finest contemporary
architects. The following year Hoffman, Gallante, and Pallasmaa began
working on the entrance design.

Dan Hoffman, a graduate of Cooper Union in New York City,
practiced architecture with William Kessler & Associates in Detroit and

taught in Canada and Italy before serving as a project architect with the office of Edward Larrabee Barnes in New York. Under Hoffman Cranbrook's architecture studio fabricated the work. Students from the Cranbrook Architectural Office, which Hoffman reactivated from 1996 to 1998, assisted in the production of the Woodward Avenue entrance and arrival features as well as in other strategic landscape interventions that Hoffman designed to complement the new construction projects. Hoffman's elegant signage and light fixtures range from low-level bollard lights made of flared aluminum tubing to petal-shaped lights for walking paths, reminiscent of reflector fittings designed by Alvar Aalto. These site furnishings are used to bring together the various roads and paths throughout campus.

Before reaching the entrance, visitors pass by several landscape features. An earth mound on the median leading up to the entrance separates traffic entering and exiting the Cranbrook campus. At the crest of the hill a soft light trough, along which are planted ornamental trees, directs visitors toward the entrance.

Beneath the winged copper-mesh canopy, the information booth nestles in the center of five supporting columns. The footprint of the information booth is *vesica piscis*, a long, pointed oval form. Its brick walls are glazed a light bluish-green similar to the stained brick on the stringcourse and watertable of Kingswood School, and its glass is tinted green. Eventually the copper-mesh canopy will oxidize to a green similar to the light green of the original oxidized copper roofs of Kingswood. The Woodward Avenue entrance seems to hover on the horizon as if about to alight. At night the structure is illuminated, its warm glow especially poignant on foggy nights. To some the structure seems inspired, in part, by a gas station. What more appropriate inspiration could there be for a structure off Woodward Avenue, in the heart of the automobile industry and the scene of the annual Woodward Dream Cruise? (The Woodward Dream Cruise is a mid-summer celebration of 1950s and '60s "cruisin'" in the place that put America on wheels.) If this is so, here at Cranbrook the base gas station is transformed into a sublime structure that heralds the entry to a campus steeped in art, culture, science, and intense beauty.

Dan Hoffman has designed a number of other features just within the Woodward Avenue entrance. His Mailbox Pavilion of 1996 is a simple cage-like shelter of vertical wooden slats that houses the mailboxes for campus residents. In 1993 Hoffman designed the Trellis Bridge. Constructed of laminated timber, the structural trellis of the bridge will eventually be covered with vines. This foot and bike bridge leads from Kingswood to the interior of the campus. Like Saarinen's two-gate entrance at Kingswood, this new entrance accommodates both pedestrians and automobiles.

At the terminus of the Woodward entrance road, between the Cranbrook Institute of Science and the Cranbrook Academy of Art and

Woodward Avenue Entrance: Trellis Bridge

Woodward Avenue Entrance: arrival feature

Museum, stands a large circular plaza known as the arrival feature. A low, curved cast-bronze wall is incised with the patterns of the stars in the northern and southern celestial hemispheres, and in the winter and summer eclipses intersects with a counter curved row of six tall slim granite columns. Each column is from a different place and each bears a latitudinal and longitudinal geographic reference to the original source of the granite; the sites refer to those areas in Canada from which Cranbrook's glacial-born rocks came. The incorporation of stars and the stones in the arrival feature symbolize science and art. Designed by Juhani Pallasmaa with Dan Hoffman and Ted Gallante, the arrival feature was built between 1994 and 1995. At the arrival feature, traffic is directed into the rectangular geometry of the center area of the Cranbrook campus. The curved configurations seem to gesture to drivers the movement of their automobiles through the plaza.

Homestead Properties

I | Cranbrook House and Gardens (Booth House)

2 | Tower Cottage, Twin Cottage, and Carriage House

3 | Greek Theatre

4 | Saint Dunstan's Playhouse

5 | Oriental Garden

6 | Italian Boathouse

7 | Mill House (Morris Mill)

8 | Thornlea House and Cranbrook Archives

9 | Hedgegate Apartments

The Booths began improving the Cranbrook property after 1904 by laying roads, grading hillsides, creating lakes, and building farm buildings. They initiated a massive planting campaign to cover the 174 acres of barren undulating land. Initially the Booths spent summers at Cranbrook in a farmhouse on Cranbrook Road known as the "Cottage," and winters in Detroit. The death of Ellen's father, James Edmund Scripps, in 1906—and the subsequent deeding of both the Scripps and the Booth houses on Trumbull Avenue in Detroit to the city of Detroit for use as a public library and park—hastened the Booths' permanent move to Bloomfield Hills.

George Booth was a man of diverse interests. He respected the skills of all kinds of artisans, loved country land, and held strong religious beliefs. Born in 1864 in Toronto, Ontario, he was one of ten children of Henry Wood and Clara Louise Irene Gagnier Booth. Booth's father, grandfather, and great-grandfather were master metalsmiths. Besides smithing copper and dealing in metal household equipment, his father worked in the newspaper business and crusaded for temperance. Booth was employed as a postal worker, a bank accountant, and then as a fabricator of ornamental iron in Windsor, Ontario, before finally entering the newspaper business. In 1887 he married Ellen (Nellie) Warren Scripps, daughter of the newspaper magnate James Edmund Scripps and Harriet Josephine Messenger Scripps at the Church of the Epiphany in Detroit, whom he had met through church activities. Ellen Scripps was a well-educated, cultured young woman with European travel. Soon after their marriage George's father-in-law, who had made a fortune providing a cheap popular daily paper to an increasing number of working class readers, appointed him business manager of the then *Detroit Evening News*.

Booth's managerial skills led to a great expansion of his newspaper domain. In 1906 he became president of the Evening News Association. Later, he bought two Grand Rapids newspapers and consolidated them into the *Grand Rapids Press*. He subsequently purchased the *Flint Journal*, *Kalamazoo Gazette*, *Saginaw Daily News*, *Ann Arbor Times News*, *Jackson Citizen Patriot*, *Muskegon Chronicle*, and *Bay City Times*, eventually—together with his brothers, Ralph Harman Booth and Edmund Wood Booth—owning and managing eight newspapers. He established Booth News, Inc.

Known for his interest in literature, nature, family life, religion, and beauty, Booth was a founding member, first president, and supporter of the Detroit Society of Arts and Crafts. His wife Ellen was a gentlewoman with many lovable and unassuming qualities, including Christian devotion and modesty. Retiring in manner, she was affectionate with her friends.

Since his youth, Booth had dreamed of being an architect. His uncle, Henry Langley, was a successful architect in Toronto, and the young Booth was said to have been impressed by his affluence. Eventually, in 1926, Booth was presented an Honorary Member Award in the Michigan Chapter of the American Institute of Architects for building well and handsomely— whether an industrial building, garage, residence, school or church. He was regarded as a man of many talents and a discriminating patron.

In Detroit the Booths and the Scrippses lived at 605 and 598 Trumbull Avenue, respectively, in houses designed by the noted Detroit architectural firm of Mason and Rice. The Scripps house was built about 1879, with later library and octagon additions. The Booth house, constructed in 1889, was a two-and-a-half story, brown brick building, on a raised foundation of rock-faced red Lake Superior sandstone. Its intersecting stepped gabled roof was covered with slate. Copper pressed in high relief covered the exterior walls of the two-story bay on the front of the house. A panel carved in high relief, showing two putti in half shell with garlands supporting a cartouche of the three-bee symbol of George Gough Booth, was featured over the decorative red sandstone entrance to the porch loggia; this ornament was rescued before the demolition of the house and transported to Cranbrook.

Landscaping, which included a pond, bridge, formal garden of mixed perennials and annuals, and a laundry yard, made the Booth property seem larger than its actual size. There was also a walled tennis court with pergola, a storage building for garden tools and large exotic trees in winter, greenhouse, and a brick horse barn with a leaded glass casement window that Albert Kahn had designed for the bay mare, Bess, the family coach and sleigh horse. For the wall surrounding the property Booth designed a gate and decorative surrounding iron work, which was executed in his Windsor shop of Evans and Booth.

Within view of both the Scripps and Booth houses, at 1519 Martin Luther King Boulevard, was the limestone Gothic Revival Trinity Episcopal Church (1890–1892, see Walk Nine Detroit). The architects were Mason and Rice, and the benefactors were Ellen Booth's parents, James Edmund and Harriet Josephine Messenger Scripps.

The Booths lived in their comfortable house on Trumbull Avenue for nearly twenty years before moving to Cranbrook in 1908. At that time the Booth house was remodeled and enlarged to nearly twice its original size for use as the Scripps Branch of the Detroit Public Library. On the garden axis was the Gothic octagon of the Scripps house, a stone vaulted library with stair tower beyond. As part of the conversion of the Booth house to the public library, the library collection was moved across the street and attached to what would become the Scripps Branch Library. With funds from the Scripps's bequest the grounds were laid out as a beautiful public garden. The Scripps Branch Library served the neighborhood until 1967, when it was demolished and replaced by the Frederick Douglass Branch Library, which opened on March 28, 1971. Scripps Park is still present at Trumbull and Grand River Avenues, but the only vestige of the former Booth house and Scripps Library Branch is the brick wall with piers running around the perimeter of the park.

The Booth family traveled from Detroit to Cranbrook each weekend until their house was built. They took the Detroit United Railway's electric interurban line north on Saginaw Road, later Woodward Avenue (Michigan 1), to Cranbrook Road or Lone Pine Road, where they were met by a driver and a two-horse coach or sleigh that transported them to "the Cottage." In good weather they drove their maroon rear-door Winton touring car. In the summer the family came out from Detroit with their gardeners and maids and stayed for the season.

For the site of Cranbrook House—their country house for their family of five children, Henry Scripps, James Scripps, Warren Scripps, Florence Louise, and Grace Ellen, in Bloomfield Hills—the Booths chose Flagstaff Hill, one of the two highest hills on the grounds of the estate. They selected Albert Kahn, also a founding member of the Detroit Society of Arts and Crafts, to prepare plans according to sketches that Booth had done. Kahn created an English Arts and Crafts house. The architect probably would have termed the rambling house English Renaissance—as he did his own house, built in 1906 at 208 Mack Avenue in Detroit, and now the Detroit Urban League (see Walk Nine Detroit). Yet Kahn's own house is really the architect's version of the prairie style with Arts and Crafts elements.

Albert Kahn was one of the most versatile and prolific American architects of the twentieth century. He designed scores of private houses, office towers, hospitals, and classroom buildings, but his innovative factory plans revolutionized industrial architecture worldwide. Kahn's factories were stronger, more resistant to fire, and with better lighting and ventilation than earlier standard designs. Born in Rhaunen, Westphalia, Germany, the first of eight children, Kahn was educated in Luxembourg. In 1880 the family moved to Detroit. In 1884 Kahn apprenticed with Mason and Rice, the firm that designed the Booth's and the Scripps's Trumbull Avenue houses. In 1890 he traveled and studied in Europe. On his return to Detroit Kahn worked for Mason and Rice, then established a firm with George Nettleton, and subsequently with Mason again. In 1902 he formed his own firm, later joined by his brothers Julius and Moritz. By the late 1910s, Kahn was not only the principal architect serving the Detroit automobile industry, but he also emerged as the premier industrial architect in America.

The contractor for Cranbrook House was the Vinton Company of Detroit, with the capable supervision of Rubin Sloan, who lived on the site with his wife during construction. In June 1908, two weeks after their twenty-first wedding anniversary, the Booths moved in. They were the first wealthy family to live year-around in Bloomfield Hills. Within four years, the Booth country estate was seen by Ella Mae Hawthorne in the *Town and Country* issue of August 24, 1912, as leading the way for the development of Bloomfield Hills, "a district of magnificent country homes with extensive, well-managed estates."

Work continued steadily on the Booth house, but most intensively between 1918 and 1922, with the addition of wings and outbuildings, the extension of terraces, and the development of gardens. Booth commissioned tapestries, wood carvings, furniture, metalwork, glass work, fine book bindings, and other decorative pieces from the workshops of leading American and European artisans and craftsmen for placement in Cranbrook House. In travels to New York, California, and Europe, the Booths selected items personally.

The Booths made lengthy sight-seeing and buying trips to Europe, sailing from New York with family, staff, and their own automobiles. During the summer of 1911 the entire Booth family, together with their chauffeur, motored through England and France. For this adventure they took with them their seven-passenger Pierce-Arrow touring car, and a Lozier Briarcliff that held four with room for another on the running board. On November 11, 1920, the Booths and their daughter, Florence Louise, embarked on a seven-month excursion trip to Europe. Closing the house for their departure took over one month because the windows had to be curtained, books covered with dust sheets, rugs rolled up, the silver taken to the vault, tapestries sent to the Detroit Institute of Arts, plumbing turned off, thermometers placed in every room, and the east wing prepared for the occupancy of the caretakers. Reopening the house for their return was the same process in reverse. From every trip the Booths brought back art and artifacts for the house, the church, the art academy, the science institute, and the schools.

The Booths built a boathouse on the south shore of Kingswood Lake and a theater and pool southwest of the house for the pleasure of boating, swimming, and theatrical entertainment. For family members and domestic employees they erected cottages near the main house.

Water was supplied to the estate through a variety of springs, wells, and two branches of the River Rouge. In 1906 workers cleared out a wooded area and dammed the Rouge to create Kingswood Lake. Water-driven ram pumps were installed at various locations around Cranbrook to supply the estate buildings. One was built at Stoney House, now a faculty residence near Kingswood. Ram House was constructed on the River Rouge across from Waterworks Cascade in 1914 to supply water to the tower behind Tower Cottage, and, in turn, to send water to the Greek Theatre pool. The

Ram House was razed in 1939 to make way for additions to Brookside
School. In 1917 Morris Mill was built as a pumping station that introduced a
heavier flow of water into the theatre pool. The mill pumps water uphill
from the millrace. From the theater pool, water cascades downhill to Lower
Grotto Lake, through the Bog Garden and a series of pools before discharg-
ing into Kingswood Lake. In turn, the lake replenishes the millrace, which
turns the overshot wheel and a pump in the lower section of the mill. In the
mid-1980s the system was rehabilitated, and the waterwheel was rededicated
on June 6, 1988.

During World War II the scarcity of heating fuel forced the Booths
to close up much of the house. They reduced their personal living space to
the Oak Room and the kitchen and to the bedrooms above these spaces.
Their son, Henry Scripps Booth, recalled times the couple would don their
coats and take their exercise by walking through the closed-off portions
of the house.

Over the years the Booths deeded Cranbrook Estate—that is, all
land except the immediate site of the house and gardens—to Cranbrook
School and to Cranbrook Foundation for the use of the five educational
institutions. Eventually, in 1944, the Booths gave Cranbrook House and its
remaining contents and surrounding property to the Cranbrook Foundation,
living out their lives there under a life trust and not as owners. The major
works of art were gifted to the Cranbrook Academy of Art; the upstairs furnishings and personal items went to the family. For some years the house
was underutilized. In reaction to the threat of demolition of the house in
preparation for subdividing the property, the Cranbrook Foundation moved
its offices into the house. Today Cranbrook Educational Community has its
executive offices on the upper floors of Cranbrook House, and the ground
floor and gardens are open to the public.

After its creation in 1973, Cranbrook Educational Community has
continued to operate Cranbrook House. In 1971 Henry Scripps Booth
formed the Cranbrook Gardens Auxiliary to preserve, maintain, and share
the historic beauty of the forty acres of grounds surrounding Cranbrook
House with the public. In 1974 a similar auxiliary was organized to assist in
preserving, improving, and extending the usefulness of Cranbrook House as
a cultural center. The two auxiliaries joined in 1977 to become the Cranbrook
House and Gardens Auxiliary with the object of preserving the house and
gardens as places of enjoyment, education, and culture to be shared by the
public. Today the auxiliary has some five hundred members. Many volunteers
are hard-working gardeners. Indeed, Cranbrook House has the largest horti-
cultural gardens maintained by volunteer gardeners of any in the United
States. Since 1974 Cranbrook House and Gardens Auxiliary has assisted
Cranbrook in the stewardship of the house and gardens, presented interpre-
tive programs, and raised funds for their restoration with its Holiday Tables

event, luncheons, tours, and spring plant sale. These volunteers maintain the furnishings and floral arrangements in the house, and raise funds for restoration of paintings, tapestries, and other furnishings. In 1995 the auxiliary formalized its commitment to Cranbrook by establishing an endowment fund to provide a perpetual source of funding for the conservation, restoration, and improvement of Cranbrook House and Gardens.

Thornlea, the Henry Scripps and Carolyn Farr Booth House, today serves as meeting space and guest housing for Cranbrook. Hedgegate furnishes housing for some of Cranbrook's faculty and staff.

Cranbrook House is the first of the great country houses built by Detroit industrialists in the early twentieth century. The house invites comparison with several in the Detroit area—two built by the Fords, one by the widow of John Dodge. Two of the three are now associated with institutions of higher learning, and all reflect these tycoons' taste for English architectural styles.

First came the Henry and Clara Bryant Ford house, Fair Lane (William H. Van Tine, 1913–1915; Jens Jensen, landscape architect, Dearborn). Originally encompassing over two thousand acres on the River Rouge, Fair Lane was the residential estate of Henry Ford and his wife Clara Bryant Ford. The large, but somewhat austere Marblehead limestone house resembles the early English or Scottish baronial style of architecture, but in fact is a blend of the late English Gothic with the Prairie style. Today the National Historic Landmark house is owned and operated by the University of Michigan-Dearborn.

The second house was for Edsel and Eleanor Ford (Albert Kahn, 1927–1929; Jens Jensen, landscape architect), at Gaukler Point on Lake Saint Clair in Grosse Pointe Shores. The stately sixty-room mansion of Briar Hill sandstone has a split stone roof. It is a superb example of the predilection of the automotive tycoons for English architecture; it reflects the cultural aspirations of Edsel Bryant Ford and Eleanor Clay Ford and their taste for great art and high-style architecture. In a departure from the elaborate palaces and fortresses favored by many of their contemporaries, the Fords engaged Albert Kahn to reproduce the comfortable Cotswolds architecture of Worcestershire, England, but on a grand scale. Formal terraced gardens, a cascading swimming pool, a deep lagoon extending from house to boathouse, and a profusion of trees and shrubs, including an "avenue of trees" landscaped by Jens Jensen, one of America's most important landscape architects, complete the setting.

The third, the Alfred G. and Mathilda Dodge Wilson estate, Meadow Brook Hall (William E. Kapp of Smith, Hinchman and Grylls, 1926–1929, Rochester Hills), was one of the last and one of the best of the great mansions built by industrialists around Detroit during the first third of the twentieth century. Mathilda Dodge Wilson, widow of John Dodge, and her second husband Alfred G. Wilson had the 110-room neo-Tudor house erected on the former John Dodge Farm, a 123-acre tract that was the site of the Dodge's vacation house until 1920. Meadow Brook Hall is a stately manor house. Its inspiration came from "ancient manor houses" in England—in particular, Compton Wynates and Hampton Court. Here, Mrs. Wilson's stable of Belgian and saddle-bred horses consumed her attention. Now the house is under the auspices of Oakland University.

1. Cranbrook House and Gardens (George Gough and Ellen Warren Scripps Booth House)

Albert Kahn, 1907–1908; H. J. Corfield, landscape architect

Library wing addition *Albert Kahn, 1918–1920*
Oak Room addition [east wing, servants' wing] *Albert Kahn, 1919–1920*

Main Entrance Gates off Lone Pine Road by Samuel Yellin, Cranbrook House

Situated on the crown of Flagstaff Hill overlooking the estate, Cranbrook House is an Elizabethan-style manor. George Gough Booth conceived of Cranbrook House as an Arts and Crafts variant of a traditional half-timbered English manor house. Albert Kahn, then a rising young architect in Detroit, designed the building. Kahn had previously built a brick horse barn at the Booth house in Detroit (on the northeast corner of the intersection of Trumbull and East Grand River Avenues). The Vinton Company of Detroit was the general building contractor. Many artists created works that became an integral part of the house: sculptors Paul Manship and Mario Korbell; silversmiths Arthur J. Stone, Elizabeth Copeland, and Omar Ramsden; ceramicists Mary Chase Perry Stratton of Pewabic Pottery and Henry Mercer of the Moravian Pottery; the Edward J. Caldwell Studio of New York; ironsmiths Samuel Yellin and Frank Koralewski; and the woodcarver John Kirchmayer of William F. Ross and Company, Cambridge, Massachusetts—all were among those who enhanced Cranbrook House through their art and craftsmanship.

The house exudes a sense of spaciousness, restfulness, and simplicity. The broad low building is constructed of concrete block with

Entrance Court, Cranbrook House

reinforced concrete floors. Glacial boulders in soft red, brown, gray, and green collected from the land form portions of the exterior walls, as well as the series of walls that surround the gardens and uphold the terraces. Smooth brick that ranges from medium red to darker purplish red laid in English bond with alternating rows of headers and stretchers rises in the exterior walls through the first story; the second story is veneered in half-timber and stucco. Chimneys with pots extend above the red-tile hipped roof, and shed dormers push out from it. Inscribed over the front carved oak door is the date 1908. A pergola now enclosed with glass shapes the sun-porch that opens onto the North Terrace.

One approaches Cranbrook House through dramatic ornamental wrought-iron gates created by Samuel Yellin of Philadelphia. From here the drive proceeds to the house along a lane of huge oak trees between two pine-covered hills. The original house is the central section of the structure. On the ground level the great central hall gives access to the reception or living room on the west, the dining room on the east, and a morning room or office on the south. Paneled woodwork covers the walls of the first floor, but on the more informal second floor, wood trim is painted white, except for the mahogany doors, and the bedroom walls are papered. The third floor originally housed guest and maids' rooms.

A three-car garage with segmentally arched openings once was located conveniently next to the house running north from the edge of the present Loggia Terrace and separated from the house by a small service court.

Wooden overmantel by John Kirchmayer, Library, Cranbrook House

Kahn created plans, aided by design sketches and input from Booth, for the addition of two richly embellished wings: the library wing and the east wing, both of which were completed by 1920. The library wing replaced what had been a pergola to the west. This was constructed just after the Detroit News Building, also by Kahn, was built in 1915–1916 (see Walk Nine, Detroit). The entire Booth family offered its comments on the library addition, and Booth's comprehensive art and architecture library served as a resource for ideas. With its shelves of hand-bound first edition books the library filled most of the wing, but the addition also contained Booth's drafting room, office, and the "still" room where he rested.

The Elizabethan style of the house was continued through the interior, and Booth ornamented it with Arts and Crafts icons. The library ceiling was plastered in a foliage motif set in interconnected squares, octagons and quatrefoils. The wooden overmantel above the huge Tudor fireplace on the west wall of the library was designed and carved by John Kirchmayer, from Booth's sketches and ideas. Born in Oberammergau, Germany, and the son of a Bavarian woodcarver, Kirchmayer expressed the true Gothic manner and spirit in his carvings and belonged to the direct line of German Gothic art. The overmantel woodcarving speaks of the ideals of the Booth family and its interest in the Arts and Crafts. In the center next to the bishop, Albert Kahn is depicted as the architect, Kirchmayer is shown as the chief sculptor, and Arthur Stone as the silversmith. Also illustrated are a metalsmith, stonemason, bookbinder, woodworker, glassblower, weaver, and others. The inscription quoted from English poet and author, Walter Savage Landor, "Nature I Love and Next to Nature Art," connects the assembly. Beneath the gathering of artisans, Christians and Muslims part company, but each group takes with it elements of the other's culture. Likewise, *The Great Crusade* tapestry of 1920 on the north wall of the library depicts America rallying to save the spiritual and cultural heritage of Europe after World War I. Conceived by Booth and executed by Albert Herter, the design features General Pershing astride a horse, as well as Charlemagne.

Kahn's other wing, the new east wing, housed the Common Room, now the Oak Room. The scene of many Booth family festivities, the Oak Room was first used for Christmas in 1920. John Kirchmayer and other German artisans handcarved the medieval linenfold-style paneling, above which are cartouches commemorating family weddings, anniversaries, debuts, holidays, and other events. A Tudor rose pattern in the plaster ceiling highlights the English manor house tradition. The fireplace, called the

Linenfold Panels by John Kirchmayer and William F. Ross and Company, Oak Room, Cranbrook House

North terrace and garden, Cranbrook House

Bible Fireplace, is surrounded by Moravian tiles from Doylestown, Pennsylvania, designed by Henry Mercer and depicting scenes from the Bible.

The west, north, and east arcades of the house front on a series of broad balustraded terraces and loggias, laid out by Burrowes and commanding splendid vistas. The spectacular West Terrace, by Burrowes and Wells, 1913, catches the setting sun. With its promenade the terrace affords an axial view to the art academy, directed by the Italian garden and linear pool and cutting through a grove to trees to focus on the *Sacred Lion Dog* statue located at the Cranbrook Art Museum. On the terrace itself "Ellen's Garden" is maintained with perennials and annuals in shades of purple. Peonies and other perennials bank the three-shell fountain. The water wheel supplied water independently at little cost to fountains and garden cascades.

The garden terraces to the north, designed in 1909, present views of Kingswood Lake and Kingswood School beyond. Here rare peonies and day and hybrid lilies surround the sundial. The Turtle Fountain, with its graceful bronze sculptures, was installed on the circular terrace in 1924. It is one of three replicas in the United States of the *Fontana Della Tartarughe* of Rome—the others being in Sarasota, Florida, and San Francisco. The fountain was restored with funds raised by the Cranbrook House and Gardens Auxiliary. Bound by a tall wall of glacial granite and reached by a divided staircase, the Sunken Garden, designed by Burrowes and Wells in 1910, today is planted with tapestries of annuals. English perennial gardens adorn the walls.

Located east of the Sunken Garden in the vicinity of the site of the "Cottage" that Henry Wood and Clara Louise Irene Gagnier Booth lived in, lies the Woodland Wildflower Rescue Garden, the brilliant and successful project of the Cranbrook House and Gardens Auxiliary. Members of the auxiliary rescue wildflowers at risk of being plowed under for development and construction. Working in cooperation with lending institutions, who identify new development projects nearby, the digging crews from the auxiliary remove the threatened plants for replanting in the wildflower garden. Surplus wildflowers are stored in a root cellar or holding garden at Cranbrook House until the annual spring plant sale. The proceeds from the sale of wildflowers in the 1999 annual plant sale amounted to $35,000, and, since the time the auxiliary added wildflowers to its plant sale inventory, over $200,000. Many of these native wildflowers furnished the plant material used in the Erb Family Science Garden at the science institute. The herb garden is located east of the former kitchen in the east wing.

Turtle Fountain, North Terrace and Garden, Cranbrook House

2. Tower Cottage, Twin Cottage, and Carriage House

Tower Cottage

> *Albert Kahn, 1908; Burrowes and Wells, alterations, 1913; Swanson and Booth, alterations, c. 1925*

Twin Cottage   *Burrowes and Wells, 1910*

Carriage House (Kennel Apartments)

> *Burrowes and Wells, 1911–1912; Henry Scripps Booth of the Cranbrook Architectural Office, alterations and rehabilitation, 1946*

Near, but separate from the family sections of the house and gardens, stands a cluster of distinctive service buildings reminiscent of a parish hamlet. These include the much-modified Tower Cottage of 1908, originally designed by Albert Kahn for Parks Walters, the family's first chauffeur. It was altered and enlarged, presumably by Burrowes and Wells, for James Scripps Booth, his wife Jean and their son, John McLaughlin Booth. About 1925 Swanson and Booth enlarged it a second time. Twin Cottage was built in 1910 for two employees. A three-unit structure, the Garage, Stable, and

Tower Cottage, Cranbrook House and Garden

Dog Kennel with Chauffeur's Quarters, 1911–1912, was designed by Burrowes and Wells, whom Kahn, by then too busy designing Henry Ford's automobile plants to do the work, had recommended to Booth. On a hillside, this banked neo-Tudor service structure was constructed of concrete block, brick, stucco, and wood. The garage had chauffeur's storage; the stables had a harness room, carriage room, horse stalls, and feed room; and the dog kennel was equipped with four individual kennels with benches that opened to a runway and a workshop for the family's beagles. The structure also held the chauffeur's quarters. In 1946 the building was converted into apartments known as the Carriage House or the Kennel Apartments. Booth's son, Henry Scripps Booth, of the Cranbrook Architectural Office, planned the alterations and rehabilitation. Today faculty and staff occupy these living quarters.

3. Greek Theatre

> *Marcus R. Burrowes (from the sketches of George Gough Booth), 1915–1916; Ossian Cole Simonds, landscape architect; Quinn/Evans Architects with Johnson, Johnson and Roy, landscape architects, restoration, 1990–1991*

The small intimate Greek Theatre, a miniature of the classical theaters of ancient Greece, was built in response to the interest of the Booths and the Detroit Society of Arts and Crafts in the Little Theater Movement. In the early twentieth century formal and informal open-air theaters were con-structed on private estates and in college grounds and city parks for com-munity performances. Most popular in the pleasant climate of California, they were also built in Michigan. Booth, who had studied ancient theaters, prepared sketch plans for the theater and pool, replicating in miniature the proportions of the Dionysian Greek Theater at Syracuse in Sicily. Located on an evergreen hilltop, the theater employs the Greek system of erecting two unconnected structures, one for the audience and the other for the actors. A pool links the two unconnected structures: the theater itself with the audito-rium, orchestra area, and stage; and an actor's court surrounded by the walls of the bathhouse. From the south, after disembarking from automo-biles at a drop-off alcove on Lone Pine Road, visitors ascend to a wrought-iron classical passage through the fieldstone wall that surrounds much of the Cranbrook Estate. From here a path leads up a slight incline beneath a canopy of crab apple trees to the auditorium. From Cranbrook House at the north, a dirt path winds through the evergreens to the theater complex.

The four-aisle semi-circular auditorium, encircled by weeping and pendulous Norway spruce and yew, holds four hundred people in five tiers of stone seats arranged close to the ample stage. The stage is elevated some four feet above the grassy orchestra area, and three openings in the stage wall give glimpses of the reflecting pool beyond. At the north end of the pool a life-sized statue of *Persephone, Goddess of Spring,* rests on her left knee with her arms and hands upraised. Sculpted by Marshall M. Fredericks in 1965, it honors Mary Alice Grindley.

Greek Theatre

Ionic pilasters and panels cast in concrete and illustrating in relief children responding to the sound of horns and drums decorate the stucco walls of the theater proscenium. The panels are casts of Donatello's cantoria sculptures in Florence, Italy. Replicas of sections from the Parthenon frieze of horses and riders adorn the wall fronting the bathhouse.

The Cranbrook Masque—written by Sidney Coe Howard, produced by Sam Hume, and presented under the auspices of the Detroit Society of Arts and Crafts—was the first play performed at the Greek Theatre, on June 26–27, 1916. Booth paid for all production costs, and the Detroit Society of Arts and Crafts made the costumes. Told in a series of episodes, the story is the triumph of romance and imaginative power over the every day world.

After its incorporation in 1915, the Detroit Society of Arts and Crafts became interested in theater arts and offered lectures on pageantry, civic drama, and stagecraft. In early 1910 May Morris, daughter of William Morris, discussed the pageant before the society. On June 24, 1910, the society staged the *Masque of Arcadia* outdoors at Claireview, the Joseph L. Hudson estate in Grosse Pointe Farms. Written by Alexandrine McEwen, the masque was produced for the simple benefit and enjoyment of those who took part in its production.

The pageant was part of the inheritance from William Morris's Arts and Crafts movement in England. The movement glorified the medieval way of doing things and represented a new interest in romance and antiquity. The pageant presented history and great literature against a proscenium of sky and trees. The Detroit Society of Arts and Crafts participated in the "little theater movement" popular in America at the time with productions. Sam Hume of Cambridge, Massachusetts, who had studied the new theater in Europe and was familiar with the new stagecraft, served as artist-director.

The little theater movement parallels the Arts and Crafts movement. Both were born in Europe, yet both were adapted to America. In America the little theater movement was a reaction to commercialism in American theater. The entertainment was presented with little or no concern for profit, but with the hope that it would cover its costs. It was given for the benefit of those who took part in it and enjoyed the artistic production of something unusual, rather that for the benefit of the audience.

The Greek Theatre is primarily a garden theater, crowning a hilltop and looking out through its evergreen hedges upon a wide vista. With the maturing of the evergreens and hedges, one is immersed in greenery and feels the power and mystery of the forest in the experience. Ossian Cole (O. C.) Simonds devised a planting scheme of 4,000 pines that eventually surrounded the theater and audience in greenery, providing a verdant backdrop for all productions.

O. C. Simonds was born in Grand Rapids, Michigan, where, on his father's farm, he developed a love of the fields and forests. As a student of civil engineering at the University of Michigan in Ann Arbor, Simonds studied architecture with William LeBaron Jenney. After graduation he went to work for Jenney in Chicago and was assigned to work on Grace-land Cemetery for that city. In Chicago he became friendly with Jens Jensen and the Prairie School of architects. Simonds considered himself a landscape gardener; he believed in studying nature as an inspiration for design, and advocated the use of native plants. He taught landscape design at the University of Michigan and was instrumental in the found-ing of its landscape architecture program.

By the 1980s, the stucco and Portland cement of the theater had crumbled, and the site was overgrown. Under the supervision of Quinn/Evans and Johnson, Johnson and Roy and with funds from the Michigan Department of Commerce, a private donor, and the Cranbrook House and Gardens Auxiliary, the complex was restored in 1990–1991. The pool now functions as a shallow reflecting pond rather than as a swimming pool, and the water still overflows down a cas-

Pool, Rear Stage and Actor's Court, and Persiphone *sculpture by Marshall Fredericks, Greek Theatre*

cade to the west. On July 21, 1991, a ceremony marked the renaming of the restored actors' court as Wonnberger Court, after longtime summer theater directors, Carl and Annetta Wonnberger. The Greek Theatre was rededi-cated on September 13, 1991, with a performance of the first play from 1916, *The Cranbrook Masque.*

4. Saint Dunstan's Playhouse (formerly Cranbrook Pavilion) *Albert Kahn, 1924; Eliel Saarinen, remodeled, 1930–1934*

The open-air Cranbrook Pavilion was built as a shelter for use in connec-tion with the Greek Theatre. Between 1930 and 1934, under the supervision of Eliel Saarinen, its open arcades were enclosed, first in glass, and later in concrete block and stucco, allowing the building to serve as an indoor

Saint Dunstan's Playhouse

theater. The concrete structure rests on a fieldstone foundation and is topped with a red tile roof. The little theater seats 206. Saint Dunstan's Theater Guild, an independent non-profit volunteer organization founded by Henry Scripps Booth in 1932 and dedicated to producing high-quality theatrical productions, operates Saint Dunstan's Playhouse.

5. Oriental Garden (formerly the Rock Garden) *1912*

Henry Wood Booth, assisted by Cranbrook's Italian-American laborers, established the Rock Garden to embellish the family gardens. During a visit to the Panama-Pacific International Exposition in San Francisco and the Panama-California Exposition in San Diego in 1915, the Booths purchased the stone lantern, three bronze cranes, and a dwarf wisteria tree to enhance the garden. Long associated with nearby Kingswood School, the Oriental Garden is maintained by the Cranbrook House and Gardens Auxiliary, whose members reconstructed the garden in the 1970s.

Oriental Garden

6. Italian Boathouse   *Marcus R. Burrowes, 1917*

Italian Boathouse (looking south from Dancing Girls *sculpture by Carl Milles and Kingswood Lake*

This masonry boathouse replaced an earlier wood-frame boathouse of 1907. The current boathouse was built for the *Nellie*, a four-oar rowboat the Booths bought from an Italian boat builder on Lake Como in Lenno, Italy. The boat served as inspiration for the Italianate style of the boathouse. To celebrate its completion in 1917, the Booths held a masquerade party, and guests danced on the roof of the boathouse. The once open loggia provided storage for canoes that were taken down the launching ramp and put into Kingswood Lake. The boathouse currently is visible from the north shore of Kingswood Lake.

7. Mill House (Morris Mill)   *1917*

Located opposite Brookside on the west side of Cranbrook Road, the Mill House, also known as Morris Mill, is a small brick structure with its overshot waterwheel constructed in 1917. It is named after an earlier mill—the Morris Mill (the Waterworks Cascade/Stiff's Flouring Mill/ Bloomfield Flouring Mill/ Old Mud Mill), built in 1828 by William Morris, the first homesteader on this

Mill House

site. The mill was one of several small businesses that Morris, his father-in-law, Amasa Bagley—who was the pioneer settler of Bagley's Corners, later Bloomfield Center—and other settlers operated in or near the vicinity of Cranbrook before the Civil War. This mill burned in 1889. The remains of the mill and such artifacts as millstones, a broken turbine, and iron shafts were on the site when the Booths acquired the property. The millpond is gone, but the remains of the race that channeled water to the mill is visible. A new waterwheel was installed in 1939. In the mid-1980s the water system was rehabilitated, and the waterwheel rededicated on June 6, 1988.

8. Thornlea House (Henry Scripps and Carolyn Farr Booth House) and Cranbrook Archives

Henry Scripps Booth, 1925–1926; Pool, 1928–1929

Thornlea comprises the main house, a gatehouse, pool, and pool house, and studios on four-and-a-half acres. Henry Scripps Booth, the Booth's youngest son, designed and built the place for himself and his wife, Carolyn Farr Booth. This house, like the senior Booth's house, was decorated with Arts and Crafts craftsmanship and art.

Thornlea is a two-and-a-half story intersecting gabled house with both shed and gabled dormers. Reddish brown brick and concrete block with brick quoins and decorative work furnish the exterior building material. The brick of the entrance pavilion is laid with a large diamond pattern. The double entry doors are set within a round archway of a pavilion. A two-story stone bay with flat roof projects from the east side. A service court and a flowing well are on the west. Radiator grilles, a windowsill, fireplace surrounds, and the walls and floors of six bathrooms were crafted with ceramic tiles manufactured by Mary Chase Perry Stratton at the Pewabic Pottery. The ceiling of the second floor oratory for family prayer was carved with Christian symbols by Oberammergau wood carvers, and the altar was once adorned with a silver cross crafted by Arthur Nevill Kirk. Today, Thornlea serves as housing for staff and guests to Cranbrook. Cranbrook Archives occupies Thornlea Studio, Henry Scripps Booth's former architectural studio to the north on Brady Lane.

Thornlea (Henry Scripps and Carolyn Farr Booth House)

Hedgegate Apartments

9. Hedgegate Apartments (formerly Hedgegate)

Marcus R. Burrowes, 1928; Cranbrook Architectural Office, remodeled, 1947

Hedgegate is a large neo-Tudor house built as a private residence for George Coleman Booth, a cousin of George Gough Booth. Hedgegate partially incorporates into its form "Italian Cottage," which was built in 1915 to house Mike Vettraino, Cranbrook's head gardener, and his wife, along with several Italian-American laborers. The Italian Cottage was the site of the Swanson and Booth architectural firm until the Art Academy Building was complete, the Cranbrook Architectural Office opened and the partnership dissolved. Hedgegate was sold to the Cranbrook Foundation in 1947 and remodeled as a faculty apartment building.

Brookside Lower School

10 | **The Meeting House**

11 | **Gymnasium**

12 | **Brookside School Wing and Log Jam Arch**

13 | **Pickle Island**

14 | **Brookside House**

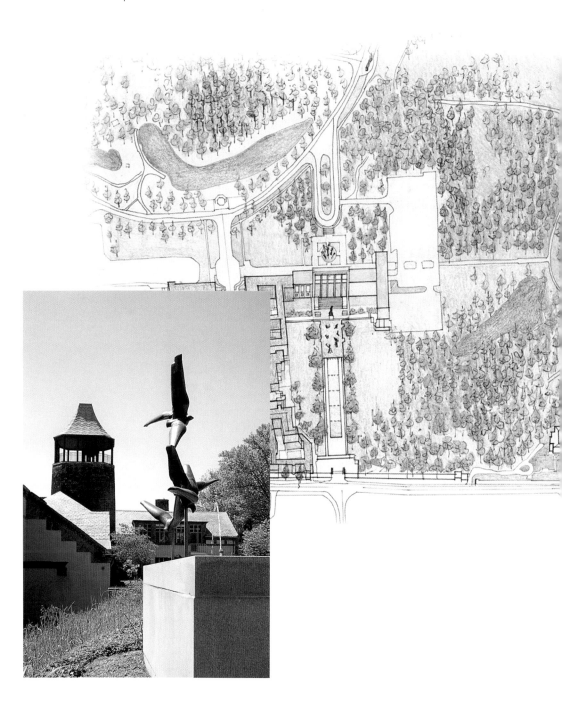

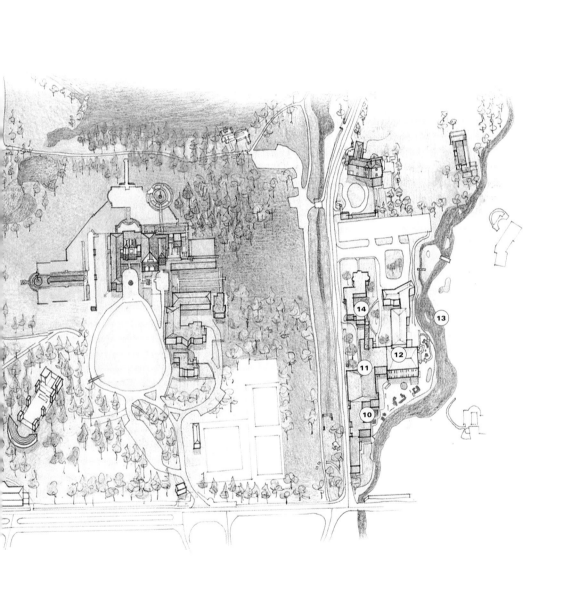

Brookside School is located on the northeast corner of the intersection of Lone Pine and Cranbrook Roads. A branch of the River Rouge flows through the eastern portion of the campus, so the long narrow site is bisected by a flood plain. Accommodating itself to its confined site along Cranbrook Road, Brookside School is a long narrow structure with a meandering train-like plan—reflecting its growth over time. Its cozy nooks and crannies, its rambling components, its maze-like corridors, and its upstairs and downstairs delight the imagination of children but often confound the orientation of adults.

Altered, added onto, and remodeled more often than any other single institutional building at Cranbrook, Brookside School is united by its Arts and Crafts flavor and its vernacular building materials—multicolored glacial fieldstone, reddish brown brick, stucco and half timber for the walls, and slate for the roofs. The Meeting House, a community building that the Booths erected in 1918, forms the oldest section and the southernmost component of Brookside School. Many additions have been grafted on to the Meeting House in subsequent years, resulting in a likeable string-like assemblage that set the aesthetic standard for the early buildings at the art academy. A gymnasium addition stands to the east. To the northeast and slightly removed from the earlier Brookside School, the New Wing of Brookside School contains the early childhood center, the science section, and the music center. The historic building has a welcoming, domestic quality that says, "Come on in!" The new wing, compatible with the old building in form, feeling, and materials, is nevertheless a product of its time.

Brookside School was the Booth's second attempt to organize a children's school. In 1912 the Booths and their neighbors decided that a school for young children was needed somewhere in Oakland County between Birmingham and Pontiac in the Bloomfield Hills vicinity. Once a farming community, Bloomfield Hills Township was rapidly growing as a place where Detroiters were purchasing large parcels of land on which to build country estates away from the noise and crowds of the city.

In September 1912, the Booths, along with William T. and Margaret Chittenden Barbour (Mr. Barbour was president of the Detroit Stove Works), John and Mary Elizabeth Booth Endicott (Mr. Endicott was a Detroit wholesaler and retailer of dry goods), Frank and Kate Agnes Thompson Bromley (Mr. Bromley was President of the Detroit Stoker and Foundry Company), and other residents of Bloomfield Hills, organized the Bloomfield Hills Seminary, soon changing the name to Bloomfield Hills School for children.

The Booths transferred to the organization five acres of property on the northwest corner of the intersection of Woodward Avenue and Lone Pine Road, including the Lone Pine Inn, formerly the Parke-Lone Pine

House built in 1830 (See Walk Eight). They contributed funds for the alteration and addition to the old house for school purposes; and the organization raised some $2,500 to finance the preparation and equipment of the school. The school opened under the direction of principal Mary Eade, served about thirty-five students, and continued educating children until World War I. In November 1918 the enrollment at the school was so low that it was closed, ending this attempt to operate a private school in Bloomfield Hills. The property reverted to the Booths, and the Booths reimbursed every stockholder for the amount originally invested in the endeavor.

Then, in the spring of 1922, a group of parents living in Bloomfield Hills and the immediate vicinity met at the Meeting House to discuss the organization of a private school for small children. These discussions led to the establishment of Bloomfield Hills School, which opened in October 1922 with Jessie T. Winter as head and sole teacher and with eight students between the ages of three and seven years. For the most part, the students were the children and grandchildren of the organizers. On October 15, 1923, the Bloomfield Hills School was incorporated. The Booths executed a fifteen-year lease of the Meeting House and the property on which it stood at one dollar a year to the school. To assist the school in meeting its financial demands, Ellen Booth began in the spring of 1924 making contributions of $500 a month from her private funds. The Booths together then followed this benevolence with the creation of the Children's School Trust on June 16, 1925, with their sons and their sons-in-law serving as trustees. They conveyed the title to the site of the Meeting House and its additions to the trust, and to the Detroit Trust Company, in trust, common stock in Booth Newspaper, Inc., the income from which was to provide for the operation of the school. The following year, in 1926, in anticipation of the future growth of the school, the Booths deeded to the Children's School Trust the balance of the property they owned adjoining the school grounds on the north. About this time, in 1927, the Cranbrook Foundation was organized, and the development of Cranbrook School was underway. On December 27, 1929, in order to maintain consistency of organization for both Cranbrook School and Bloomfield Hills School, the trust document was amended to provide for a board of directors to operate the school, with the title to the property remaining in the Children's School Trust.

Subsequently, in 1930, to avoid confusion with the Bloomfield Hills public schools that had been incorporated in 1927 using the same name, the name was changed from Bloomfield Hills School to Brookside School Cranbrook. Thus, in 1931, Brookside School opened and reorganized as a school for young children on the country day plan. Jessie T. Winter, the headmistress, explained in a letter to the Booths on May 11, 1932: "The reorganization of Brookside this past year on the Country Day plan, with longer hours, more supervised play and a definite emphasis on an activity program, has allowed more opportunity for integration–education of the whole child. Believing education to be not a mere accumulation of habits, facts and skills, but real living, we have redoubled our efforts to allow our students freedom for growth—scholastically, physically and socially, under wholesome, stimulating conditions. We have brought the world into the school, and we feel, from enthusiastic reports our students are taking the school into the world."

Today five hundred day students are enrolled at Brookside School from pre-kindergarten through grade five. Many attend before and after school care as well.

10. The Meeting House

George Gough Booth with Henry Scripps Booth, 1918;
George Gough Booth and Henry Scripps Booth, additions, 1923, 1924, 1925;
Henry Scripps Booth, Main School Building Addition and Tower, 1928–1930;
Henry Scripps Booth, addition, 1939

Library   *1964–1965; Crossings, remodeling, 1990s*
Multipurpose Room *Crossings, remodeling, 1995–1996*

The Meeting House is a fieldstone and brick Arts and Crafts building with half-timbering and casement windows. It resembles an English farmhouse. It was built between June and late fall of 1918 as a center for social, instructional, political, and religious gatherings for the community.

The first religious service was held in the Meeting House in January 1919. This service was conducted by George Booth's father, Henry Wood Booth, who earlier had organized a Sunday school and gathered together the boys and girls from the countryside in a tent on the nearby hilltop at the southeast corner of the Booth property. With the construction of the Meeting House, religious services and Sunday school were held at Cranbrook on a more regular basis, and movies were shown here on Saturday evenings. In 1922 the Meeting House became Brookside School. It remains the most intact of the old school components.

Over the fireplace of the simple hall, Katherine McEwen, a founding member of the Detroit Society of Arts and Crafts, who would later do the fresco at Christ Church, painted a mural that reflects the prevailing hope held by people during the wartime years for a brighter future. Beneath the Star of Bethlehem, one of the Three Wise Men holds an astrolabe in his hands as if to tell of the "New Earth" in the same manner as the wise men of 1918 looked to the future for the hope of the world. McEwen also painted the trusses and the ceiling. Born in Detroit, the great granddaughter of Judge Solomon Sibley, McEwen studied painting in Germany and lived in England for a while, absorbing the Morris Arts and Crafts movement. John Kirchmayer carved representations of the four Evangelists—Matthew, Mark,

Meeting House and First Additions, Brookside School

Luke, and John, as symbolized by the angel, lion, eagle, and ox—in the corbels of the supporting roof trusses. Above three casement windows opposite the fireplace is inscribed, "The sovereignty of man lieth hid in knowledge wherein many things are reserved which kings with their treasure cannot buy." The stage at the south end of the Meeting House was added after 1930.

To the Meeting House, by then operating as Brookside School, the Booths built three additions, creating what many have called the appearance of a series of storybook cottages. They were constructed in the summers of 1923, 1924, and 1925, and subsequently altered, remodeled, enlarged, and partially removed to make way for yet other additions.

To accommodate the expanded enrollment, William Smith built a two-story stone addition in 1923. Mother Goose characters—Mother Goose Flying to the Moon, Peter Pumpkin Eater, Jack and Jill, and others— carved by Joseph Jungwirth adorn the oriel window. Inside, five stained glass windows featuring child-like representations of music, dance, geography, drama, and mathematics, admit light to a classroom that was formerly a little study hall. The first floor contained a study/art room, the second floor a faculty apartment, the ground level classrooms.

Music Stained Glass Window, Former Little Study Hall, First Addition to Meeting House, Brookside School

Named for the water-driven ram pumps in the basement, the stone and stucco "Ram House" addition, built as enrollment reached thirty-nine in 1924, included an apartment (once occupied by the architect J. Robert F. Swanson), and offices for the school doctor, psychologist, and others. A small dining room addition was built north of the old Ram House to the plans of Henry Scripps Booth in 1925.

As Brookside School added grades and expanded to over one hundred students—boys from kindergarten through sixth grade and girls from kindergarten though tenth grade—it needed still more space. The short-lived dining room addition of 1925 was removed in 1929 to make way for a new fireproof main school building, constructed to the north.

The tower is the signature element of the historic Brookside School. Before the completion of the new arrival area north of the New Wing, one approached Brookside School from Cranbrook Road by proceeding east between entrance posts surmounted by cherubs and dolphins into a small courtyard. The school was entered through the double doors in the base of the tower. Above the main entrance, four blue and white tiles depict the four seasons. Made at the Wiener Werkstätte, these tiles were purchased by George Booth at the Decorative Arts Exposition of Paris in 1925. Through a second tower, smaller in diameter but connected to the main tower at the south, a spiral staircase climbs sprightly to an open belvedere on the main tower with a steeply pitched, ridged, and flared pavilion-hip roof. Part way up, the stair tower opens to a full-size room in the main tower, but the ascent itself and the belvedere at the top indulge one's fantasies of power. From this height captivating views of Brookside abound. In creating the tower, Henry Scripps Booth remembered what it is to be small and hoped to give the children a sense of presence in their world.

The River Rouge was diverted, and the Ram House addition removed in 1939 to create space for a classroom addition for the first three grades. Three stories in height, it was designed by Henry Booth. A pair of ram's heads from the 1916 Rainbow Fountain, placed here to mark the earlier presence of the Ram House, peers down on the meandering lower level room. The frieze of the gabled entry displays nursery rhyme figures carved in wood and painted: the Old Woman who lived in a shoe, Mary and her lamb, and others.

The library occupies the light, airy former glassed-in courtyard, now enclosed and open to the sky with skylights. Just above a child's eye level wonderful original illustrations from children's books line the walls. Blue faience tile lines the former courtyard fountain, and three sculptures crouch within it. The wall fountain was designed by Henry Scripps Booth to include a sculptural relief of a pelican and baby chicks, which Geza Maroti had carved in 1927 for the tympanum over the main entrance to the south

Library interior with Pelican and Chicks *by Geza Maroti, Brookside School*

lobby of Hoey Hall at Cranbrook School, but which was never installed. Crossings, a firm of the former students of Dan Hoffman, executed the renovation of both the library and the multipurpose room. Formerly used as the senior kindergarten room, the multipurpose room is large high-ceilinged room used as a gym, lunch room, and performance space. Open trusses support the roof, and from the high ceiling hang ten brass chandeliers. A stage projects from the south wall.

The space within Brookside School has been rearranged, and the building improved, repaired, and remodeled in a variety of ways between 1961 and 1980 to accommodate new methods of teaching children. Heating, ventilating, air conditioning, and other mechanical improvements have also been made. Nevertheless, the historic features and nooks and crannies of the rambling, maze-like school remain intact to capture the imagination of its students. Corner classrooms, for example, still retain their defunct fireplaces, framed by tiles with images of animals and airplanes.

11. Gymnasium *Tom Hewlett of O'Dell, Hewlett and Luckenbach, 1959–1960*

The Cranbrook Foundation commissioned the construction of the large gymnasium. It was dedicated to former headmistress, Jessie T. Winter, in honor of her many years of service to Brookside School.

12. Brookside School Wing and Log Jam Arch

Brookside School Wing *Peter Rose, 1995–1997*
Log Jam Arch *Dan Hoffman and the Cranbrook Architectural Office, 1997*

By the late 1980s Brookside Lower School was bursting at the seams. The demand for admission to the school continued to increase, and educational programs were expanding. Brookside specifically needed an early childhood center and space for science and the performing arts. The planning and construction of a new wing at Brookside Lower School comprised one of the five major new projects at Cranbrook identified in the master plan.

Peter Rose, the architect of the new wing, was born in Montreal in 1943, educated at Yale University, and is adjunct faculty at the Harvard

Graduate School of Design; he has offices in Boston and Montreal. His design of the Canadian Centre for Architecture (1984–89), a museum and study center in Montreal, demonstrated to the Cranbrook Architectural Advisory Council his ability to sensitively incorporate new construction with an historic landmark building. The Centre project received the American Institute of Architect's National Honor Award and represented Canada at the 1991 Venice Biennale. Moreover, Rose's plans for fine private houses that complement their natural environment and create warm interior spaces impressed the council. Of Brookside Rose noted:

> Brookside School, whether by accident or design, is persistently irregular, composed of parts that are rather small in size and scale. Full of surprise and delight, it seems to exist primarily and properly on children's terms—as if adults may be there by consent. Further, I have been struck by the symbolic and real power of the site—located between one of man's most powerful marks, the road, and one of nature's most beautiful creations, the stream—wonderful fertile ground on which to educate children.

Rose's plan for the new wing responds to the small size and scale, the irregularity, and the child-like qualities of the historic Brookside buildings, as well as the River Rouge flood plain that bisects the site. Rose noted that Brookside School moves deftly through three zones, from wild nature on the east to civilized natured in the middle, to civilized chaos on Cranbrook Road and the west.

The new wing comprises three sections: the Vlasic Family Early Childhood Learning Center for three-to five-year old children, the science rooms, and music rooms. The sections are joined by a window-lined walk-

Brookside School

Brookside School Wing (looking northeast from Tower)

way, and, taken as a whole, the wing adds 20,410 square feet to the school. Standing apart from the historic school, the Brookside School Wing runs to the north along the brook, its mass creating courts. Indeed, the wing and its position relative to the historic school and former headmistress's house create a court within a court, reminiscent of Saarinen's courts at Cranbrook School and the art academy. A flood wall protects the building from the threat of rising water.

Steel and concrete blocks, wooden beams, trusses, and decking make up the building materials of the new wing. Ranging from pale brown to gray, the made-to-order concrete blocks are masterfully laid in the walls so that an occasional block is recessed or projected in the manner of skin-tled brickwork. Wherever a concrete block is broken or cut, brick quoins are laid. The use of concrete blocks in such an eminent building as the new wing is borrowed from Henry Scripps Booth's elevation at Thornlea, one door north (see Walk One). Slate cov-ers the skylight-punctuated hip roof. The chimneys are steel. Lead-coated copper is used for all metal that pro-trudes. Steel windows are set in wood casings. The doors are steel, and steel forms the balcony off the music room. Students impressed hand prints in concrete on the exterior of the new wing to personalize the school and to recognize donors.

Children's Handprints, New Wing, Brookside School

Kindergarten Room, Brookside School Wing

In keeping with its mission of providing a private, nurturing space for very young children, the Vlasic Family Early Childhood Learning Center is somewhat removed from the areas of Brookside the older students use and has its own separate canopied entrance, created by the Cranbrook Architectural Office. The Early Childhood Center is scaled to child size. Here children can see out the windows at their own eye level, and counters, cubby-holes, reading nooks, and window seats are well within their reach. Child-size metal lockers—designed with unusual cut-outs to help the youngest students identify their lockers—and a wall of windows, under which are metal radiator covers perforated in decorative patterns, line the corridors of the new wing. Naturally finished wood panels suspended from the ceiling conceal the electrical system and can be removed for repair work. *Our Brookside* (1996–1997), a tile terracotta mosaic panel of squirrel, bee, dragonfly, frog, turtle, and rabbit figures—the animals one is likely to encounter on the Brookside campus—decorates the full west wall of the lower hall at its intersection with the hall to the historic Brookside School. Created by a team of art teachers, the mosaic includes the fingerprint of every student at the school at that time.

Shed roofs and two-story classrooms differentiate the science rooms from the rest of the wing. Two new science classrooms nearly double the space formerly allocated to science, providing all Brookside students with space for experiments, plants, and animals. Double doors open outside to the brook, and high glass ceilings to the sky, connecting the students with the natural environment.

At the south end of the new wing a large open music studio rises two stories and accommodates full ensemble groups; the mezzanine holds an office, and a balcony overlooks the River Rouge. The walls of the room are lined with rectangular wood panels seamed with wooden strips, and the ceiling with skylights. The *Hymn to Brookside* is inscribed in a panel of the south wall. In addition to this large studio, the mezzanine provides student musicians with a smaller studio for string ensembles and for study and practice.

Music Room, New Wing, Brookside School

A new entrance off Cranbrook Road serves as a proper courtyard that civilizes the connections between the car and the school. Older children entering must walk through Log Jam Arch, a log pergola designed by Dan Hoffman and the Cranbrook Architectural Office.

Because the Brookside wing is sited on former playing fields, both the lower and upper playing fields have been moved to the west side of Cranbrook Road and are accessed through a tunnel built beneath the road.

Brookside's new wing is harmoniously woven into Cranbrook in a way that responds to the values of the Booths and Saarinen. The design

Log Jam Arch, New Wing, Brookside School

acknowledges the scale and rhythm, craftsmanship, and additive quality of the historic school, and is a recognizable product of its time.

Pickle Hut and Brookside School Wing

Bridge and Pickle Island and Pickle Hut, Brookside School

13.   Pickle Island

The Bridge to Pickle Island   *Dan Hoffman and Cranbrook Architectural Office, 1997*
The Pickle Hut   *Dan Hoffman and Cranbrook Architectural Office, 1997*

In the course of the construction of the Brookside School Wing during
1995–96 the enlargement of the water course to serve as a flood control

device created Pickle Island in the middle of a branch of the River Rouge. A wood plank footbridge with bent steel railings topped with a wooden handrail connects the Brookside School site to Pickle Island and its Pickle Hut. The hut is a wonderfully mysterious, U-shaped, shingled teepee hideaway in which children seek playful shelter, tell stories, and dream. The kiva-like structure was built in 1997. The island was named in honor of Robert J. Vlasic, the founder of Vlasic Pickles and long active in the school as a trustee and member of Cranbrook's governing board.

14. Brookside House (formerly the Headmistress's Residence)

Henry Scripps Booth of the Cranbrook Architectural Office, 1929–1930

Brookside House is reportedly one of the first tri-level houses erected in Bloomfield Hills. Designed with entrance hall, reception hall, living room, dining room, kitchen, study or office, maid's room, and four upstairs bedrooms, the house was first occupied by Cranbrook Headmistress Jessie T. Winters. It currently houses administrative offices.

Brookside House (Headmistress's Residence)

Christ Church Cranbrook

15 | Christ Church Cranbrook
16 | Rectory
17 | Sexton's House

15   16   17

Christ Church Cranbrook, the property of the Protestant Episcopal Church of the Diocese of Michigan, stands apart from the Cranbrook Educational Community but is linked to Cranbrook historically. It was built to serve as a spiritual cornerstone for the entire Bloomfield community of faculty, staff, workers, and students at the Cranbrook institutions, along with their families and neighbors.

When the Booths came out from Detroit to their Cranbrook property on weekends, they began attending Sunday morning religious services in Birmingham. First, in 1904, they went to Saint James Church, later the Presbyterian Church, and then returned to Saint James Church. In Detroit the couple had met and been married at the Emmanuel Reformed Episcopal Church, later named the Epiphany Reformed Episcopal Church—the predecessor of Trinity Episcopal Church (Mason and Rice, 1890–1892, see Walk Nine).

Since 1904, Henry Wood Booth had preached to over one dozen neighbors in a tent pitched on the bluff overlooking the intersection of Cranbrook and Lone Pine Roads. In January 1919 the elder Booth began conducting services in the Meeting House, which is today Brookside Lower School. The gift of the Meeting House to Bloomfield Hills School in 1922, however, made the plans to erect a church more urgent.

On October 4, 1923, Booth wrote to the Reverend Samuel Simpson Marquis, D. D., former Dean of the Cathedral Church of Saint Paul in Detroit and then Rector of Saint Joseph Protestant Episcopal Memorial Church (now the Roman Catholic Church of the Holy Rosary), about the need at Cranbrook for "a good church building delightfully located, attractively furnished, and provided with facilities for good music." Booth favored the site at the intersection of the corner of Lone Pine and Cranbrook Roads diagonally opposite the Meeting House. His letter sought Marquis's approval for his proposal and inquired if Marquis might consider a post in the center of such a project. In a second letter to Marquis Booth stated, "We are prepared to set aside several hundred thousand dollars for the erection of a good church building with a school adjoining or detached, and to provide a residence for the Rector, a yearly income. . . . "

A graduate of Cambridge Theological School, Samuel Simpson Marquis served as rector of Saint Joseph Protestant Episcopal Memorial Church in Detroit from 1899 to 1906, and again in 1922. In 1906 he became dean of the Cathedral Church of Saint Paul in Detroit, overseeing its monumental construction between 1908 and 1911 by the architect Ralph Adams Cram (See Walk Nine). In 1915 Marquis headed the Welfare Department of the Ford Motor Company, which was dedicated to aiding the many immigrant workers at the Highland Park Plant of the Ford Motor Company and their families in adjusting to life in the United States, by providing English language courses and guidance on budgeting, health, and insurance.

In this manner, Booth obtained the interest and support of Marquis and the concurrence of the Right Reverend Herman Page, bishop of the diocese of Michigan, that the Cranbrook church would form part of the Episcopal diocese of Michigan. In 1924 Bishop Page officially established the unorganized mission of Bloomfield Hills and appointed the Reverend Samuel Simpson Marquis, D. D., missionary-in-charge of the new parish. (Later he would become rector.) Then the bishop named a building and grounds committee and a finance committee to move ahead in the development of the church. The building and grounds committee consisted of Booth, his architect son, Henry Scripps Booth, and Marquis.

As members of the buildings and grounds committee, the Booths and Marquis paid serious attention to their work. Henry Booth, who graduated from the University of Michigan's architecture college in 1924, served as the family's design liaison with the architects, but many family members freely proposed ideas for gifts they would make to the church. Marquis provided iconographical schemes for the church and selected scriptural passages from the Bible for painting or carving into the church. George Booth himself participated in the design and oversight of construction and corresponded directly with many of the artists commissioned to work on the church.

As architect for the church complex, Booth sought one of the best church Gothicists in America: the talented firm of Bertram Grosvenor Goodhue of New York. Goodhue was an active member of the Boston Arts and Crafts Society. He worked on the art of typography and book design. He designed the Cheltenham typeface and *The Altar Book* (1896), printed by Daniel Berkeley Updike's Merrymount Press, the American counterpart to William Morris's Kelmscott Press, after which Booth had modeled his Cranbrook Press. At age fifteen Goodhue had left his home in Pomfret, Connecticut, for New York City to work in the offices of the gifted Gothic church designer and architect of the Smithsonian building, James Renwick. With the unexpected death of Goodhue, Booth turned to his associates—his former partner Ralph Adams Cram, and Oscar H. Murray, a principal in Goodhue's firm. After pointing out to Booth that it was unethical to ask two architects simultaneously to prepare preliminary sketches, Cram reportedly bowed out of the competition for the proposed project, and Booth offered the commission to Bertram G. Goodhue and Associates, since he had been working with Murray. Murray of the Goodhue firm served as chief architect and designer of Christ Church.

Charles R. Wermuth and Son, of Fort Wayne, Indiana, was the general contractor. The contract to build Christ Church Cranbrook established an ongoing relationship between Wermuth and the Booths at Cranbrook.

Christ Church Cranbrook, together with the rector's and the sexton's houses, is sited on a four-acre tract of land known as South Cranbrook on the River Rouge at the southwest corner of the intersection of Lone Pine and Cranbrook Roads. Between the sexton's house and the River Rouge is a little spring-fed lake, affectionately called the Sea of Galilee. This site had several advantages over other locations that were considered. Situated at an intersection of roads, only a mile from Woodward Avenue, the South Cranbrook property offered access from all directions. The rolling contour to the land presented a gentle slope rising to the west, and the site had ample space for the church, other buildings, and parking. Today the church lies between Cranbrook Educational Community and the residential neighborhood to the south. Cranbrook has held graduations, convocations, and other ceremonies at Christ Church, and Samuel S. Marquis served as the spiritual advisor for the school and representative on advisory boards.

15. Christ Church Cranbrook

Oscar H. Murray of Bertram G. Goodhue Associates, 1925–1928; porch addition, 1928–1929; Percival Gallagher of the Olmsted Brothers, landscape architect, 1926–1928

Community Hall/Parish House (formerly the Guild Hall)

Oscar H. Murray, 1925–1928

Church School and Administrative Wing

Mayers, Murray and Phillip, 1937–1938

Christ Church Cranbrook is a towered late Gothic Revival stone structure designed in an interpretation of English Gothic Revival parish churches. Booth assembled a team of the country's leading contemporary Arts and Crafts artisans and craftsmen to create the building, ornamental detail, and church appointments. In fact, Christ Church is the last major collaborative effort of the country's leading Arts and Crafts workers.

At first the Booths felt they wanted a simple country church, something in the form of a chapel that would seat about two hundred people. Very early on Booth had drawn a sketch for the church that was similar in form and arrangement to but smaller in size than the final executed design. In Booth's plan the church was to connect with a future school. The architect Oscar H. Murray felt that the severe and formal church sketched by Booth would be out of place in its rural surroundings. The men did agree

Christ Church Cranbrook, west façade

that the church should be Gothic, however, inspired by the old churches Booth had admired in the English countryside of Kent. To reduce costs and to maintain quality they eliminated the school for the boys' choir. Booth formulated other ideas instead for the boys' school on the farm site west of the church. Some thought was given to adding a Roman Catholic chapel to the church, but financial considerations forced the Booths to scale the building back to a single church. The tower and ell connected a wing containing the community hall, dining room, and kitchen.

Booth had anticipated expenses in the amount of $650,000 for the construction of the church, community hall, and rectory. But the bids came back well in excess of that amount. When bids were let a second time, Wermuth and Son came in with the lowest cost. The firm separated the work, decoration, and furnishings into three areas: the construction of the church and the rector's and sexton's houses; the interior woodwork of the church, including oak screen, stained glass windows, hardware, decoration of roof, pews, and the like; and special furnishings, such as chancel decoration and tapestries. The total came to just under one million dollars. Because Wermuth was the low bidder and because the firm had executed another stone church for Goodhue, they were awarded the commission for Christ Church.

Ground was broken on July 5, 1925, and the cornerstone laid on June 26, 1926. Speaking at the laying of the cornerstone ceremony, Bishop Page said: "This is a cornerstone not only of a church but of several other closely related institutions. It is significant that the cornerstone of the church is laid first. There is profound reason for this. A church stands for that which is highest and noblest in life."

As the foundation was being laid, Booth became concerned that the church would be too small to accommodate the growing Birmingham and Bloomfield Hills communities. Before the west wall of the front was completed, he added two bays to the west end of the structure. The lengthening of the nave not only added space in which to seat worshipers, but also heightened the dramatic view of the chancel and the high altar from the narthex.

With construction underway, Booth and his family selected artisans to provide carved woodwork, stained glass, frescoes, sculpture, mosaics, tapestries, and metalwork. Many family members made gifts of furnishings, most of which were designed by the architects. On September 29, 1928, the church was consecrated.

In 1929 a porch giving access to the narthex was added, the gift of Clara Louise Gagnier Booth in memory of her husband Henry Wood Booth.

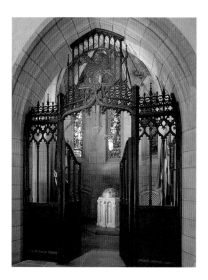

Baptistery (Chapel of Saint John), Christ Church Cranbrook

Chapel of Saint Dunstan, Christ Church Cranbrook

At the north end of the narthex is the baptistery, also known as the Chapel of Saint John. Gothic arcades separate the side aisles from the lofty narrow nave space, which progresses beneath a hammer-beam timber roof to the choir and chancel, uninterrupted by a transept. The north aisle opens to the Chapel of Saint Paul. A square carillon tower rises over the library, formerly the vestry, at the intersection of the nave and the community hall wing. The sacristy, treasury, church store (formerly the parlor), library, and robing room are arranged off the small hall that connects the entrance to the community hall and church proper. The chapels of the Resurrection and of Saint Dunstan lie beneath the chancel in the area the vaulted stone crypt would occupy, if it had been executed. An extending ell to the south contains the community hall, formerly the guild hall, with its meeting room on the upper level and dining room and kitchen on the lower level.

Chapel of the Resurrection, Christ Church Cranbrook

Built during the spring and summer of 1938, the wing housing the church school and administrative offices lies to the southeast. This two-story stone addition has large windows and a flat roof that respectfully permits an unobstructed view of the church from the south. Mayers, Murray and Phillip, the successor firm to Bertram Goodhue Associates, designed the addition.

Across the rolling lawn is the rectory, and beyond, next to a little wooded spring-fed lake known as the Sea of Galilee, is the sexton's house.

Christ Church is executed in light grayish Berea, Ohio, sandstone with whitish gray Bedford limestone trim. Its rough-cut, exterior walls, slate-clad roof, and high-style Gothic forms celebrate the social, cultural, and economic achievements of Cranbrook and Bloomfield Hills. Twelve elongated stone figures, carved on site by Edward Ardolino after designs by Lee Lawrie, depict Wilbur Wright, inventor and pioneer aviator; Louis Pasteur, chemist and developer of pasteurization and the technique of vaccination; Michael Faraday, English scientist and developer of the first dynamo and formulator of electrolysis; Nicolaus Copernicus, Polish astronomer; Galileo, Italian astronomer, mathematician and physicist; and Leonardo da Vinci, Italian artist; among others. The figures of Mary and John placed on the bellcote at the northeast corner over the chapel were sculpted by Ulric Ellerhusen.

Great traceried stained-glass windows are positioned over the main west entrance and on the east wall of the chancel. The west window is dedicated to womankind. The gift of James Alfred and Florence Louise Booth Beresford, it was designed by James H. Hogan and executed by James Powell of London, England. In each of the sixteen panels, three women illustrate an area of service, skill, or art: motherhood; Christ's associates; early missionaries, early saints, members of religious orders; American church missionaries; educators; nurses; musicians, artists; novelists; sovereigns; painters, poets; liberators; and suffrage workers and actresses. The women are represented by such people as Mary, mother of Jesus; Mary Magdalene; Mary Lyon, founder of Mount Holyoke College; Clara Barton; Mary Cassatt; Louisa May Alcott; Emily Dickinson; Harriet Beecher Stowe; and Sarah Bernhardt. The east window, over the high altar, depicts scenes from the life of Christ in twelve medallions. Executed in brilliant blues, reds, and greens, it is the work of Nicola d'Ascenzo of Philadelphia and the gift of Henry Scripps and Carolyn Farr Booth. The clerestory windows, with grisaille glass created by G. Owen Bonawit, admit soft but ample light.

To the north of the narthex is the baptistery, the Chapel of Saint John. Its vaulting ribs are supported on stone corbels carved with aquatic figures, and the ceiling is covered with sparkling iridescent Pewabic tile mosaics created by Mary Chase Perry Stratton and set in a tree design. The base of the font and the random square tiles in the floor are paved with Christ Church Cranbrook tile fired at the Pewabic Pottery. Leo Friedlander sculpted the octagonal base of the baptismal font with female figures symbolic of fruits of the Holy Spirit in Siena marble alternating with mosaic panels. The exquisite copper and enamel cover to the baptismal font was

*West window (*Womanhood *by James H. Hogan), tapestries, and narthex screen, Christ Church Cranbrook*

designed and executed by Edward F. Caldwell and Company, of New York, under the supervision of Victor F. von Lossberg. It displays children of the four races of man in prayer in the gardens of the world with their native flora and fauna. The baptismal font won the 1928 Gold Medal of Honor in Native Industrial Art from the Architectural League of New York.

In addition to the baptistery, Christ Church Cranbrook has three chapels (Saint Paul's Chapel, the Chapel of the Resurrection, and the Chapel of Saint Dunstan). To the north of the nave Saint Paul's Chapel (the Chapel of Paul, the Apostle to the Gentiles) seats 56 people beneath a stone vaulted ceiling. The reredos, painted by Hildreth Meiere of New York, depicts the progression from the Law of the Gospel as typified on the three mounts: Sinai, Calvary, and Mars Hill. The center panel shows the crucifixion of Christ with criminals on either side on Mount Calvary; the panel on the left illustrates Moses giving the Ten Commandments to the people of Israel, and the one on the right shows Paul preaching to the Athenians at Mars Hill. Below the panels are pictures of some of Jesus' parables. The prophets—Isaiah, Hosea, and Amos on the left and Mark, Matthew, and Luke on the right—were sculpted by Alois Lang and divide the three panels. The chapel is dedicated to all workers in missions and charities.

The Chapels of the Resurrection and Saint Dunstan are located beneath the chancel in the space the vaulted stone crypt usually would occupy. The former is fitted with an altar of black and pale brown Italian marbles in decorative panels. Mosaic pavement in the chapel depicts a peacock with its tail outspread, a symbol of the resurrection. The mosaic was designed by Oscar H. Murray, chief architect of the church, and executed with Italian marbles. The painting is *Descent from the Cross*, by Francis Scott Bradford. Pilgrims interested in Cranbrook's arts and crafts history must be sure to experience Saint Dunstan's Chapel because it is dedicated to the patron saint of artists and craftsmen.

The east window, executed by Harry Wright Goodhue of Boston, features Jesus as the central figure, holding three nails and a hammer, symbols of his crucifixion; Joseph, the carpenter, on the left, with a saw; and Noah, the shipwright of the Old Testament flood, on the right. Beneath are the shoemaker, musician, and metalworker. The north window shows Bezeleel, the Old Testament jeweler; Saint Dunstan, archbishop of Canterbury and patron saint of the artist craftsman; Fra Angelico, monk and painter; John Kirchmayer, woodcarver; and Bertram Grosvenor Goodhue, architect. Poignant memorial tributes to craftsmen who worked at Christ Church and Cranbrook are carved on columns: Eliel Saarinen and Oscar H. Murray, architects; Gaetano Vettraino, gardener; Albert Leipold, stonecarver; and Arthur Nevill Kirk, silversmith.

Katherine McEwen, a founder of the Detroit Society of Arts and Crafts, painted the chancel's stunning fresco. Booth had requested that she elaborate upon the little group she had painted over the fireplace in the Meeting House. McEwen prepared sketches for the fresco in 1926 at Seven Dash Ranch, Johnson, Arizona, to which she had retired, because of the "inspiration of the mountains," rather than at Cranbrook. She did the color work at Cranbrook, however, selecting a little more vivid tones than one might think appropriate so as to hold up against the brilliant stained glass and the gold of the window the painting surrounds. The soft oranges, gold leaf, pale green, light bluish green, blue violet, and rose indeed seem inspired by the colors of the desert. "If I could only transfer one of our sunsets to the walls it would stand up against any stained glass," McEwen wrote to Booth in 1926. The fresco is notable for its lovely airy color, its fine craftsmanship, its excellent spacing and composition, and for the successful way in which it has been felt as an integral part of the wall. She took as the theme of the fresco the building of the church throughout the world, from the words, "He hath built his church on the foundation of the apostles and prophets," in the Epistle to the Ephesians, which appear at the base of the painting. The left side depicts the aggressive church, the right the realm of ideas rather than action. The earthly church is at the bottom and the celestial choirs above. The evangelists flank the altar; Peter and Andrew are on the north wall, the archangels, Michael and Gabriel, on the upper east wall, and behind them the four beasts of the apocalypse before the Lamb of God. The black cat below the stone niche on the south wall may be McEwen's symbol for her name or simply a portrait of her companion.

The huge tapestries high on the south and north walls of the narthex portray the "old dispensation," or rule of law, and the "new dispensation," or rule of love. They were designed by the English artist J. H. Dearle, and executed by Morris and Company of Merton Abbey, England.

Irving and Casson-A. H. Davenport Company of Boston carved the intricate oak traceries above the side aisle stalls on the north side of the nave and the oak screen that separates the nave from the narthex. Glass overlaid with ornamental leading was hand wrought by G. Owen Bonawit of New York and installed within the narthex screen. The great doors of the organ case on the south wall of the nave

Oak Screen by Irving and Casson overlaid with ornamental leaded glass by G. Owen Bonawit, Narthex, Christ Church Cranbrook

were created by Alfred E. Floegel of New York. They were the gift of James Scripps and Jean McLaughlin Booth. The hammer-beam roof was decoratively painted by Floegel.

John Kirchmayer carved the high altar reredos with its figures of Christ—triumphant, presented in the temple, and as an infant; he also

Door by John Kirchmayer, South Choir Aisle, Christ Church Cranbrook

carved the door off the south choir aisle leading to a meeting room off the vesting room, formerly the office of Dr. Marquis, depicting Doubting Thomas and the craftsmen who contributed work to the church— Koralewski, Hogan, Goodhue, d'Ascenzo, and Kirchmayer himself; and he carved the magnificent west doors in the Chapel of the Resurrection, portraying angels swinging censers. Ecclesiastical accessories—chalice and patten, crosses, candlesticks, and a binding for the *Book of Common Prayer*—were smithed in sterling silver and sumptuously inlaid with semi-precious stones, crystals, enamel, and ivory by Arthur Nevill Kirk.

The fifteen-panel oak treasury door, richly bound and trimmed with pressed and tooled metal, was designed and crafted by Oscar Bruno Bach. Figures of angels, singers, prophets, and evangelists and Christian symbols decorate the strong door to the storage room beyond that keeps safe the rare and beautiful precious objects.

The women of the parish stitched the needlepoint kneelers in the 1960s. Four of the kneelers illustrate the central focus of life: rest and recreation, love and nurture, order and justice, and work and service.

The craftsmen tucked in several whimsical notes. For example, the fanciful wood carvings on the ledges under the seats in the back row of the choir stalls include a view of Booth and the architect Oscar Murray pulling the church apart, marking the decision to increase its size.

Intermingled with Arts and Crafts works are historic art treasures from Europe. The fifteenth-century bishop's chair came from the vicinity of Amiens, France. The eighteenth-century sanctuary lamp in Saint Paul's Chapel was made in Florence, Italy. The terra-cotta relief with three singing angels over the side-aisle exit from the nave to the community hall was done by Giovanni della Robbia. The marble candlestick in the narthex is a replica of Paschal Candlestick in the Capella Palatine, Palermo, Sicily.

Nave (looking east), Christ Church Cranbrook

The tower of Christ Church boasts a carillon, an unusual musical instrument that originated in the lowlands of Belgium and Holland. It consists of at least twenty-three bells, hung stationary on a frame, which are rung by means of wires from a keyboard and pedalboard—operated by the carillonneur using his fists and feet. Although a centuries-old tradition in the Old World, carillons did not really arrive in the United States until the 1920s. Christ Church Cranbrook's carillon, the gift of Harold Wallace and his family, represents one of the earlier concert instruments to be installed in America, and as such would have signalled the sophistication and cosmopolitan nature of Cranbrook's congregation. The forty-six bells were cast by the English bellfoundry John Taylor of Loughborough, and the carillon was dedicated in 1928. Two more bells were added in 1929 to give the carillon four chromatic octaves. In 1975 the family of Grace Booth Wallace provided funds for recasting thirty-five of the top range bells by improved methods, and they were installed in 1978.

Christ Church projects the intent of George Gough Booth and Ellen Warren Scripps Booth: "The only way to have is to give, the only way to keep is to share, and the only thing worth finding is opportunity." At home the Booths found and acted on an opportunity and, thereby, presented another opportunity to others.

Percival Gallagher of Olmsted Brothers prepared a planting plan for the vicinity of the Christ Church wall around the property. Booth told the Olmsted firm that he favored fairly heavy planting around the houses of the rector and sexton and comparatively little planting about the church itself. The firm selected and ordered plants and supervised the execution of the landscape plans. The separateness of Christ Church from the rest of Cranbrook and the widening of Lone Pine Road limited the firm's role in the landscape. It replaced some large-canopied trees with smaller trees, many shrubs, and assorted perennials for flowerbeds. A columbarium was installed in the north garden of the church in 1978; a larger columbarium was built in 1984–1985.

16. **Rectory** *Oscar H. Murray of Bertram G. Goodhue Associates, 1925–1928*

The gabled stone rectory is compatible with the stone church. One enters onto a large hall with access to the rector's study and the living room and the dining room. This arrangement enables the rector to conduct private conferences and small social events with little disruption to the household.

Rectory, Christ Church Cranbrook

Sexton's House, Christ Church Cranbrook

17. Sexton's House   *Swanson and Booth, 1926*

The tiny masonry, fieldstone and wood-frame residence stands slightly removed from the rectory and the church, reflecting the lesser position of the caretaker of the church. Today the associate rector lives in the house.

Cranbrook Kingswood Upper School

18 | Main Entrance Gate (Peacock Gate)

19 | Cranbrook School Quadrangle

20 | Hoey Hall and Tower

21 | Alumni Court (West Court)

22 | Thompson Oval and Stadium,
Lerchen Hall, and Keppel Gymnasium

23 | Williams Natatorium

24 | Marquis Hall, Page Hall, and Stevens Hall

25 | Dining Hall

26 | Infirmary

27 | James C. Gordon Hall of Science

28 | Music Building

29 | Faculty Way Houses

30 | Valley Way Houses

31 | Cranbrook Boys' Middle School Campus

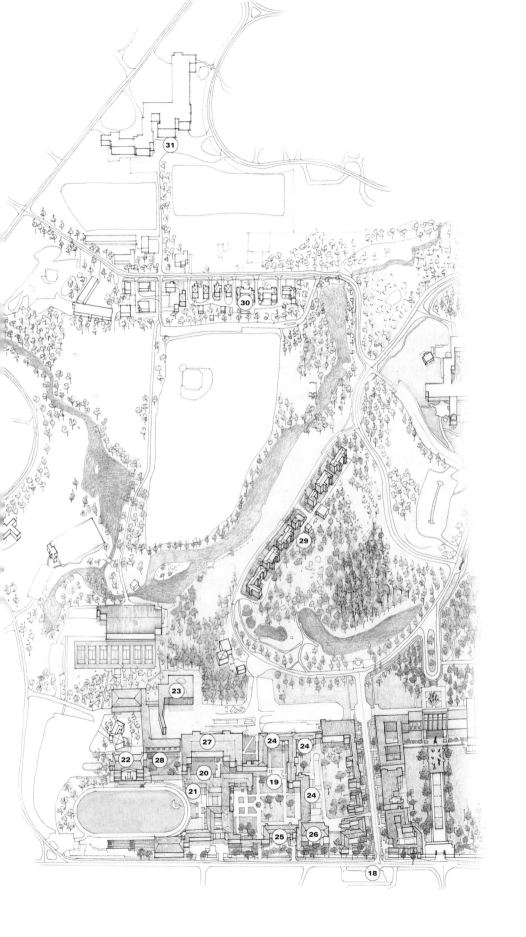

The Former Cranbrook School for Boys

Cranbrook School was first conceived as a boys' choir school connected to Christ Church Cranbrook. Since there was a need for a small school for boys in Bloomfield Hills, and since it was thought that a boys' choir might be required for the church, one school might serve to satisfy both needs. George Gough Booth eventually determined that a larger school would be preferable—one not connected with the church and one as far as one-quarter or one-half mile away from the church that cost less to build and have room for playing fields. The Booths decided to establish a pre-collegiate school for boys at Cranbrook, some students of which might sing in the choir of the church.

Cranbrook School was founded to provide for the intellectual training and the moral and religious education of the youth in its care. The donors wanted the school to benefit by the best traditions of similar undertakings in the past and the clearest visions of the future. They wished that the school would demonstrate a spirit of progress and an open-mindedness in education and religion. To shape educational policies and to manage secular affairs, they would enlist qualified, experienced, and competent people. Though not limited to any particular religion, the school, by its relationship with Christ Church Cranbrook, was to be associated with the Episcopal Church. The curriculum would offer a good general education and provide competent instruction in drawing, design, decoration, and the artistic handicrafts. With the general purpose of the school to make good citizens, the Booths contemplated in what kind of buildings this best should be accomplished.

The sixty-five-acre parcel of land designated for Cranbrook School was the site of a dairy farm, where Booth had built good quality farm buildings on a large scale in 1911, with the design assistance of Marcus R. Burrowes, who followed his architectural sketches. By 1926 Booth had given up farming and sold off his herd of Guernsey cows and other livestock. The land lay fallow, and the farm buildings stood unoccupied, but they were clean and in good working order.

Booth and his architect son, Henry Scripps Booth, studied reusing and remodeling these farm buildings for the school. The younger Booth, with his friend, J. Robert F. Swanson, also recently graduated from the architecture college at the University of Michigan, developed a complete campus plan that called for remodeling the buildings and locating playgrounds. Thus, Swanson and Booth were engaged to convert the farm to school use after the senior Booth's designs. And Eliel Saarinen was hired as a consultant. After Swanson's marriage to Pipsan Saarinen in 1926, Swanson and Booth broke up; the firm was renamed Cranbrook Architectural Office, and Saarinen became chief designer.

In the hands of Eliel Saarinen, who by then was at Cranbrook, the plans for the school took off and presented a campus of thoroughly and

Cranbrook School (looking northeast)

beautifully remodeled farm buildings. As Booth described in a 1937 memorandum about the founding of Cranbrook, "Where the silo had stood was a fine [octagonal] tower with an observatory on top. The former hayloft became a first-class assembly hall." Foundations were improved, walls faced with brick, and tile replaced shingles on the roofs.

Charles R. Wermuth of Fort Wayne, Indiana, the builder of Christ Church Cranbrook, won the contract for the construction of Cranbrook School. He found that he could submit a lower figure for a completely new building than for a remodeled structure. The architects accordingly revised the plans, positioning the buildings in a manner almost identical with the arrangement of the former farm buildings. The academic building stands on the footprint of the hay barn; the tower was where the silo had stood; the study hall, library, and library workshop sit on the footprint of the wagon shed, the implement house, and the blacksmith shop; the arcaded court had been the barnyard. Hoey Hall, formerly the Academic Building, opened first. Later the dormitories, athletic buildings, dining hall, and kitchen went up. The half-timber building that served as dairy and farm workers' quarters was remodeled as a faculty residence.

Saarinen was experienced in planning on a large scale. After winning second prize in the international competition for the Chicago Tribune Tower design, Saarinen and his family traveled from Helsinki, Finland, to Chicago. Here, from his apartment in Evansville, Illinois, in 1923, Saarinen worked on a monumental scheme for the lakefront development in Chicago that presented solutions for traffic congestion. Again, in 1924, in his proposed development project for the Detroit Riverfront at the foot of Woodward Avenue, Saarinen created solutions to traffic congestion with a

Eliel Saarinen with his wife, Louise (Loja) Gesellius Saarinen, an accomplished designer who oversaw the textile and weaving department in the Cranbrook Academy of Art; Cranbrook Archives

triple-decked esplanade and subway station and automobile parking under the decks. Tackling the campus plan and design for Cranbrook was a challenge Saarinen could meet.

Cranbrook School represents the first completed architectural work of Eliel Saarinen in America. The historic complex consists of exquisitely crafted brick buildings topped with steeply pitched red-tile-clad roofs grouped around a quadrangle, courts, and terraces in the manner of English collegiate quadrangles. Although the general character of this group recalls medieval cloistered monastic and collegiate complexes, the stylistic character is the result of a creative synthesis using abstract medieval motifs and Finnish romanticism, an eclectic mix of contemporary Scandinavian work in the spirit of Ragnar Ostberg and Martin Nyrop, and European art nouveau. In his design work Saarinen combines excellent technical ability with unequaled craftsmanship.

Cranbrook School reveals the architect's roots in the Arts and Crafts movement—and specifically the Vienna secession style—that flourished after 1897 with its ideal "the total work of art." Indeed, Cranbrook is a total work of art. The whole includes buildings, landscaping, sculpture, paintings, furniture, dishes, and silverware. For Cranbrook boys school, Saarinen won the Gold Medal Award of the Architectural League of New York for 1934.

While still in Europe, Saarinen had traveled and studied with the Hungarian artist Geza Maroti, a proponent of the Arts and Crafts. Seeking an artist capable of working compatibly with him to design the decorative detail of the Cranbrook buildings, Saarinen suggested to the Booths that they invite Maroti to Cranbrook to create the sculptural ornamentation of Cranbrook School. Bringing in Maroti reflected Saarinen's belief in the integration of art and architecture—a philosophy that was very influential in the development of Cranbrook's philosophy. Albert Kahn so admired Maroti's art embellishment and sculpture at Cranbrook that he arranged for him to do the ceiling of the lobby of the Fisher Building in Detroit in a stylized pattern and brilliant colors. The Fisher Building was Kahn's most important non-industrial building of the 1920s, and the lobby ceiling a Maroti masterpiece.

The early Cranbrook prospectus stated, "Cranbrook aims to stimulate in the boy industry, originality, initiative, and responsibility both as to his own concerns and as to the community in which he lives. Every effort will be made to develop the spirit of democracy which is inherent in American boyhood." Unexcelled for its completeness and for its artistic conception, the Cranbrook campus was a community in itself. With its spaces for academics, athletics, sleeping, eating, and religious services, it was deemed an ideal place in which to meet these lofty goals.

As stated in their current prospectus, Cranbrook Schools-Cranbrook Kingswood Upper School seeks "to prepare young men and women from diverse backgrounds to develop intellectually, morally and physically; to move into higher education with competence and confidence; and to appreciate the arts." The schools also strive "to instill in students a strong sense of social responsibility and the ability to communicate and contribute in an increasingly global community."

Although the school buildings were conceived to accommodate 200 boys, Cranbrook School opened in the fall of 1927 with 74 students in seventh, eighth, and ninth grades, one-third of which were boarders, and a faculty of eleven. Each year thereafter a grade was added until all institutions offered full preparation. The first students came from Birmingham, Bloomfield Hills, Pontiac, Detroit, and Grosse Pointe. Cranbrook Kingswood Upper School was formed in 1984, when Cranbrook School for boys and Kingswood School for girls merged. By the year 2000, 740 day and boarding students from twenty states and eighteen foreign countries were enrolled in the Cranbrook Kingswood Upper School.

In his 1927 presentation address at the Cranbrook School Dedicatory Exercises Booth explained, "We were unwilling to go through life with our aims centered mainly in the pursuit of wealth and with a devotion wholly to the ordinary opportunities for social satisfaction. We were not willing to leave all of the more enduring joys for our children or the joy of work in so good a cause entirely to our friends after we had passed on; rather did we wish, in our day, to do what we could and give tangible expression now to our other accomplishments by adventures into a still more enduring phase of life. We wished to see our dreams come true while we were, to the best of our ability, helping to carry on the work of creation."

William Oliver Stevens was selected as Cranbrook's first headmaster. Stevens was born in Rangoon, Burma, to a family of educators. He received his B.A. degree from Colby College in Waterville, Maine, and his Ph.D. degree in literature from Yale University. An educator, author, and artist, he taught at the Naval Academy in Annapolis for twenty years and served as headmaster of the Roger Ascham Country Day School near White Plains, New York, for three years. Under the tutelage of Stevens, the Cranbrook School community set out to establish standards for conduct and accomplishment and to create customs, traditions, and policies to match the architecture.

The school needed publications, emblems, colors, and symbols. The titles of its publications, *The Crane* for the school newspaper and *The Brook* for the school yearbook, were derived from Crane Brook, the river that flows near the town in Kent, England, for which the school was named. The school colors of royal blue and gray followed the idea of a "Nation United" after the Civil War, but they were also the colors of Colby College, the alma mater of Headmaster Stevens. School spirit meant supreme teamwork. In observation of the dress code and the code of conduct students dressed and behaved as young gentlemen. The school initiated Founders' Day and Christmas pageant traditions.

18. Main Entrance Gate (Peacock Gate)

Eliel Saarinen and Oscar Bruno Bach, 1927

Main Entrance Gate off Lone Pine Road (Peacock Gate), Academic Quadrangle, Cranbrook School

The ceremonial entrance to the Cranbrook School Quadrangle and Cranbrook School is through the Main Entrance Gate (Peacock Gate) off Lone Pine Road. The iron gate was designed by Eliel Saarinen and manufactured by Oscar Bruno Bach, a German-born metalworker. Bach studied at the Royal Academy in Berlin and belonged to the Architecture League. Peacock figures and the words, "Cranbrook School A.D. 1927," adorn the upper portion of the gate, and a dragon is fashioned into the latch handle. The gate is hung in a gabled brick archway that parallels Lone Pine Road. In a recessed niche above, flanked by multiple varied arched niches, rests a stone eagle with head turned to the west. The gate anchors the main north/south axis of the quadrangle, which runs to the Quadrangle Fountain, on to the Gateway of Friendship, and terminates beyond at the automobile drop-off for the Williams Natatorium.

19. Cranbrook School Quadrangle

Eliel Saarinen, 1926-1929; C. De Forrest Platt, landscape architect

The Cranbrook School Quadrangle is defined by four groups of school buildings: Hoey Hall (the Academic Building and Tower) on the west; Stevens Hall on the north; Page and Marquis Halls on the east; and the Dining Hall and two surviving historic farm buildings on the south. The quadrangle and the adjoining courts and terraces are approached through archways and paths. The ground is paved with wide flagstones laid with brick set in patterns and is sodded between walks.

The Cranbrook School Quadrangle is an open, rather than an enclosed, equilateral cloister. Openness suggested a more sympathetic attitude to the world outside the school than the closed English collegiate quadrangles and cloistered medieval monastic quadrangles.

Both this quadrangle and the Alumni Court were restored during "The Great Restoration," a Cranbrook Alumni Council campaign in the early 1980s. The architects Tarapata/McMahon/Paulsen (TMP) recreated original patterns in brick and stone, matching colors and textures. But exterior walkways, terraces, and courtyards of brick are difficult to maintain

Quadrangle Fountain and Hoey Hall and Tower, Cranbrook School

in the harsh Michigan climate, and by 1999, the brick had deteriorated again. At this printing, there are plans to restore the walkways according to standards and techniques established in the restoration of the nearby Auto Court to the south.

Occupying the center of the Cranbrook School Quadrangle, where it is the focus of the north/south axis from the Main Entrance Gate to the Gateway of Friendship, is the Quadrangle Fountain. Erected in 1927, it is a replica of the fountain in the corner of the cloister of the Monreale Cathedral in Palermo, Sicily. Its Carrara marble shaft with chevrons cut in a stepped edge and topped with a global finial is decorated with full human figures and heads of animals that spew water from their mouths. The shaft rises above a base and basin of travertine. Booth purchased the fountain in 1927 from the Chiurazzi Foundry in Naples, Italy, for some $7,000. Eliel Saarinen designed the basin for the lower pool and the steps leading down to it, as well as the three-section concrete benches that wrap around the east side of the fountain.

Before Tower Court facing the Cranbrook School Quadrangle is the *Aim High* sculpture, crafted in 1972 by Peter Kerr, a former art instructor at Cranbrook School, after an Eero Saarinen design. Saarinen based his archer on a story in Virgil's *Aeneid* in which Acestes, the fourth archer contestant,

Armillary Sphere *sculpture by Paul Manship, Cranbrook School*

shot his arrow high into the sky, and the gods, pleased with his spirit, tipped his arrow with fire so that he won. The *Aim High* image appears on the school seal.

On the northwest quadrant of the quadrangle, just outside the bay window of the library reading room, which contains a large globe, is the *Armillary Sphere*. One of several created by Paul Manship, who designed the *Prometheus* at Rockefeller Center in New York City, an armillary sphere expresses the ancient Greek conception of the universe. The symbols of the zodiac in relief march along the broad circumference band that represents the equator, and the names of the zodiac, which tell of the rays of the sun shining on the rotating earth, are inscribed on another encircling band. The bar that goes through the center of the sphere casts a shadow on the widest band, marking the time on Roman numerals. The bronze sphere is mounted on a circular base that is supported on the backs of twelve turtles. Figures of a man, woman, and child rest on the circular base. The ancient Greek astronomers used these spheres as teaching devices. Alexis Rudier Fondeur of Paris manufactured the object, and the Booths purchased it from Scott and Fowles of New York in 1926 for $5,000.

20. Hoey Hall (formerly the Academic Building) and

Tower *Eliel Saarinen, 1926–1928; Tower, Eliel Saarinen, 1928–1929*

Hoey Hall contains classrooms, library, study halls, assembly hall, and administrative and faculty offices for Cranbrook School. It is arranged with rooms off a wide central hall and with several wing additions for class-rooms, arts and crafts, and administrative offices. The building was con-structed as the main academic building of the boys' school. Today, all upper school classes are held here.

Hoey Hall and other early buildings at Cranbrook, with the excep-tion of Christ Church, are constructed with structural steel and reinforced concrete fireproof floors. The dark orange-red common brick, uniform in shape and size, is laid in the exterior walls in common bond, in which every sixth row consists of headers, the other courses being stretchers. Red clay roofing tile, known as Brittany shingle tile and manufactured by the Ludowici Celadon Company of Chicago, covers the exterior surface of the steeply pitched roofs.

The main entrance to Hoey Hall is just south of the tower. The door opens onto the ample, well-worn, welcoming south lobby of the Academic Building, named in honor of Harry D. Hoey, teacher and the fourth head-master of Cranbrook School from 1928 to 1964. Behind a shuttered counter, once the switchboard for the school, is now the office of the dean. The brown tile chimneypiece of the huge fireplace on the north wall is embell-ished with five tiles of football, tennis, basketball, and baseball players and a track runner, designed by Eero Saarinen and fired at Pewabic Pottery in Detroit. These sports figures in the main academic building proclaim at once the integration of athletics and academics at Cranbrook. Here, in the lobby, once hung Benjamin West's monumental painting, *The Death of Wolf*. The painting now graces the walls of the Common Room of Page Hall. Pipsan Saarinen Swanson painted the geometric decoration in brown, sil-ver, and gold on the poured concrete ceiling beams. Passing through the south lobby to an exterior walkway supported upon the arcade of Alumni Court, one may descend stairs to the athletic oval and stadium on the west.

The two-tiered octagonal tower off the south lobby, which forms the centerpiece of the Hoey Hall composition, rises to a small dome that once held the observatory. The telescope did not work well in the tower, because

Galileo portal by Geza Maroti, Hoey Tower, Cranbrook School

the heat waves rising from the surrounding chimneys and the formation of ice on the dome's interior from condensation in winter interfered with its function. In 1931 the instrument was moved to the institute of science.

The lower level entrance to the tower, known as the science door, is through the Galileo portal. The limestone entrance pierces the rusticated Berea sandstone wall of the tower adjacent to Tower Court. The sandstone may have been leftover from the building of Christ Church. Galileo stands on a pedestal above the portal. Geza Maroti carved Galileo as well as the representations of astronomy, invention, physics, geology, geography, and biology in the panels of the portal's piers.

If one climbs the tower's spiral staircase to the second floor, which contains the 250-seat assembly hall, one passes the *Diogenes* sculpture by George Edwin Bissell. From his position on a pedestal projecting east off the second floor landing of the tower, *Diogenes* stands, lantern in hand, looking for an honest man. The Booths purchased the sculpture in 1914 from the Gorham Company of New York.

The wood-paneled lobby of the assembly hall on the second floor features ornament representing exploration and discovery, a theme also treated in the north lobby. Installed high over the fireplace is the painted *Columbus Window* by the stained-glass company of G. Owen Bonawit. Bonawit described in a letter to Henry Scripps Booth of April 28, 1927, his proposed design for the window, which follows Booth's suggestion: in the center of the composition is the figure of Columbus in blue, rose, and red, globe in right hand, in front of his ship, the *Santa Maria*, in black and gold " . . . so as not to be conspicuous and also lend a very fine decorative background feeling." Underneath is a label with the words "Christopher Columbus." A map of Columbus's first and second voyages is in the base. A small painted insert on the left bottom shows Columbus landing on Hispaniola. It is from a wood cut of 1493, supposed to be after a drawing by Columbus himself. The two shields contain the Coat of Arms of Columbus and Spain. Booth in his response to Bonawit on June 10, 1927, said, "We want the window to appear as much as possible in one plane, eliminating as much landscape and suggestion of distance as you can. Also the figure itself we would like very much conventionalized. Mr. Saarinen, the architect does not wish to introduce a semi-antique suggestion in this window, as the building is quite modern in feeling."

The Assembly Hall accommodated the student body for morning chapel services and for assemblies. Removable rows of wooden chairs arranged on a flat floor beneath a barrel vaulted ceiling faced the stage and altar. A large brick hearth and fireplace with inglenooks cozily tucked beneath a balcony is the heart of the lofty beamed entrance lobby.

Assembly Hall Lobby, Hoey Hall, Cranbrook School

Painted on one lobby wall is a *Map of North America Depicting the Principle Expeditions of Discovery and Exploration* (1928) by John Hession, Jr. The map illustrates the salient historical and natural features of this continent and portrays the major early voyages and expeditions.

The study hall and library wing of Hoey Hall is perpendicular to the hall on the north. This wing was built on the site of a farm storage building. Today the study hall and library are combined as a resource center with computers, book stacks, and reading room.

Doorway by Geza Maroti, Study/Library Hall, Cranbrook School

A wild-haired human head representing "knowledge," carved in relief in wood by Geza Maroti, surmounts the original junior study hall door. This is surrounded by carved fruits of the harvest—squash, wheat, corn, grapes, and the like—and flanked by free-standing fluted stone columns.

The word "Library" with the image of an open book surmounts the diamond patterned wooden entrance to the library. Inside, the central panels of the three library doors are enhanced with painted glass panels, the subjects of which George Gough Booth left to G. Owen Bonawit. One is an old printer's mark—the mark of Galliot Du Pré, a French painter of the sixteenth century. The others show the printer's mark of Jacob Stadelberger. The barrel vaulted reading room of the library is arranged with a fireplace and cozy inglenooks for readers on the west wall, a bay window on the opposing east wall, and windows on the north wall. Bookshelves line the walls from the floor to the ceiling.

Library interior, Cranbrook School

Geza Maroti designed the limestone chimneypiece in 1928, which is entitled *The Gift of Knowledge*. It features two quotations: "The Fear of the Lord is the beginning of knowledge," and "Culture is to know the Best that has been said and thought in the world." The figure of knowledge is at the top center, flanked by figures of Youth, and Mother and Child. Below on tablets in smaller and lower relief, images chart the history of man, as it was conceived in America in the late 1920s, from Adam and Eve to the voyage of

Columbus. Between these symbolic figures are small tiles reserved for mottoes appropriate for the library. "Religion, Morality and Knowledge Being Necessary to Good Government And the Happiness of Mankind, Schools and the means of education shall be forever encouraged" from the Northwest Ordinance of 1787 reminds the reader of the role of education in making good citizens.

21. Alumni Court (West Court) *Eliel Saarinen, 1927*

West of the main campus group on the original site of the farm's hog and bull pens is Alumni Court, with the Thompson Oval and stadium beyond. Formed by the west walls of Hoey Hall and two classroom wings, Alumni Court cloisters a small yard with its double columned arcade. For the capitals alumni created designs "to be approved by Mr. Saarinen and Mr. Price." On the shafts the names of

Pankration *sculpture, Alumni Court, Cranbrook School*

graduates from the classes of the 1930s and 1940s are inscribed, giving the court its name. The centerpiece of the garden is the *Wrestlers*, a sculpture installed in 1929 illustrating the Olympic athletic contest in which men fought to the death. Tarapata/MacMahon/Paulsen (TMP) restored the courtyard in 1987. Stairs descend from Hoey Hall and its additions to the Thompson Oval, stadium, and Lerchen Hall.

Stairway from Alumni Court to Thompson Oval and Stadium, Cranbrook School

22. Thompson Oval and Stadium, Lerchen Hall (formerly Little Gym), and Keppel Gymnasium

Thompson Oval and Stadium *Eliel Saarinen, 1928*
Lerchen Hall, formerly Little Gym *Eliel Saarinen, 1927–1928; remodeled, 1932*
Keppel Gymnasium *Eliel Saarinen, 1929–1930*

Cranbrook School Football *relief sculpture by David Evans, Thompson Stadium vicinity, Cranbrook School*

Thompson Oval is named after Paul "Admiral" Thompson, a former athletic director of Cranbrook School. A running track encircles the football field. Saarinen's innovative stadium seating scheme built into the south hillside has inspired several comparable plans at other campuses.

Overlooking the playing field of Thompson Oval is a sculptural relief cast in bronze in 1930, illustrating scrimmaging football players. The school's first team, comprising freshmen and sophomores, posed for the panel, but the English artist, David Evans, was unfamiliar with the game, and the players appear clumsy and awkward. The *Discus Thrower* and *Hermes,* bronze copies of classical sculptures by Myron and Lysippus, frame the golden oak doors to the

Discus Thrower and Hermes *sculptures, Lerchen Hall, Cranbrook School*

former Little Gym; the Booths purchased the sculptures in 1930. These doors were added when the gym was converted to a performing arts building in 1932.

Keppel Gymnasium, completed in 1930, is named for Charles J. Keppel, a Cranbrook faculty member from 1927–1935 and first dean of students at Cranbrook School. With its brick exterior walls, oxidized copper-clad roof, and telescoping chimney stack, the building forecasts Kingswood. A long north/south corridor and locker rooms connect to the gymnasium at the north. The gym is encircled with a suspended track.

23. Williams Natatorium

Tod Williams and Billie Tsien, architects, 1998–1999; Peter Osler, landscape architect

By the 1990s athletic programs at the Cranbrook Schools had outgrown their physical facilities, and there was still no swimming pool. For practice and meets Cranbrook Kingswood swimmers traveled to school pools in nearby communities. Cranbrook trustees decided to build a new athletic complex to meet the needs of students and to serve as a recreational center for the entire community. Williams Natatorium, 20,000 square-feet, is a superb recreational, competitive, and instructional indoor swimming pool. It is the first executed phase of a larger athletic complex to be completed in future years.

The Cranbrook architectural advisory council recommended Tod Williams and Billie Tsien to design the natatorium, because of the firm's experience in planning swimming pools, and because of its unusual ability to create compatible and sensitive contemporary additions to historic buildings. A graduate of Cranbrook School, Tod Williams studied architecture at Princeton and Cambridge Universities. Billie Tsien has fine arts degrees from Brown, Yale, and the University of California at Los Angeles. Based in New York City, Williams and Tsien have designed extraordinary buildings on two of America's most distinctive campuses: Feinberg Hall at Princeton (1987) and New College at the University of Virginia (1992). They were also the architects for the downtown branch of the Whitney Museum of American Art in New York City (1987) and the Neurosciences Institute in La Jolla, California (1995).

The natatorium is sited on a hillside just east of Keppel Gymnasium. Connecting to the gym by an enclosed bridge and forming a courtyard with the Gordon Hall of Science, this spectacular new structure proudly anchors the east/west axis that extends from the west terrace of Cranbrook House to the east facade of the natatorium. Integrating athletic life with academic life, the architects elevated Williams Natatorium to the level and stature of Hoey Hall.

Brick of warm earthy colors, glazed to a dull iridescent finish, and panels of bluish green glazed brick rise in the exterior walls to a cornice

Williams Natatorium, swimming pool, Cranbrook School

Williams Natatorium, corridor, Cranbrook School

band of pale bluish green glazed brick. The exquisite colors recall the sky and the pool water, as well as the oxidized copper roofs, the trees, and the ground. The building is trimmed in bead-blasted stainless steel, aluminum, zinc-coated copper, and mahogany woodwork. Lightly sandblasted concrete and concrete block in dark reddish purple that is sand-cast with iridescent aggregate chips in red, gold, pale yellow, gray, and brown and ground-faced forms the interior walls.

A long ramped connecting corridor with a switchback runs north/south to link the east entrance, the swimming pool hall with its spectators' stands, the Keppel entrance, and the locker rooms. In the corridor opposite the east entrance a light bay of sandblasted plate glass panels projects into the hall, admitting light to the space. To the north a light pier filters natural light down to the upper hall and the boys' locker room below. A perforated aluminum light shield runs the full length of the ramped corridor.

The swimming pool is set in the very heart of the building. The stucco ceiling is a striking cobalt blue, with twinkling round lights of varying diameters. The colors are extraordinary: dark grayish green, slip-resistant slate tile lines the deck of the pool; Spanish glass tile mosaics line the interior. Cantilevered viewing galleries and stands along the edge are large enough to seat two hundred on mahogany and gray slate benches. Hand-cut, hand-glazed ceramic tile lines the shower walls of the locker rooms.

Williams Natatorium is a building that does something unexpected. It practically merges with the outdoors. Mahogany louvered wall panels can be hydraulically powered to swing open. Huge picture windows, though stationary, permit views of the woods. Two elliptical oculi in the ceiling can be retracted to reveal the sky. The oculi are reminiscent of the unglazed eye in the coffered dome of the ancient Pantheon in Rome. Like the Pantheon, the Williams Natatorium exudes its own spirituality. The architects—through the use of dramatic color and materials and by opening the pool to the sky and the woods—have evoked what it feels like to be young and have fun. In fact, the only reason not to open the pool to the outside is the possible entry of birds that might roost among the wires, hangers, and ducts above the dropped ceiling. But a metal bird screen effectively keeps them out.

Marquis, Page, and Stevens Halls, Cranbrook School

24. Marquis Hall, Page Hall, and Stevens Hall

Marquis Hall (formerly the Junior Dormitory) *Eliel Saarinen, 1927*
Page Hall *Eliel Saarinen, 1929–1930*
Stevens Hall (formerly the Senior Dormitory) *Eliel Saarinen, 1927–1928*

The three interconnected dormitories were built sequentially on the northeast corner of the quadrangle. Together they had rooms for two hundred students and apartments for thirteen unmarried and five married masters. Marquis Hall is named for the Reverand Samuel Simpson Marquis, Rector of Christ Church Cranbrook and ex-officio member of the Cranbrook School Board of Directors. On the south side of Marquis Hall, Marquis Arch links Marquis Hall and the Dining Hall. Designed by Saarinen, the archway gives entry to the Cranbrook School campus and the quadrangle. It is at the termination of a walkway leading from the Cranbrook Academy of Art to the north of the infirmary. "Cranbrook School A. D. 1927" is inscribed on the east side of the exterior arch; "For the Development of Growing Youth" on the east side of the interior arch; "A Life without Beauty is only Half Lived," George Gough Booth's guiding philosophy underlying

"A life without beauty is only half lived (George Gough Booth)," Marquis Arch, Marquis Hall, Cranbrook School

the school on the west side of the interior arch; and "Truth Leads to Beauty as Sparks Fly Upward" on the west side of the exterior arch. The inscriptions, all by Booth, speak of the inspiration and ideals of the school. An intricate stone and timber pergola, also designed by Saarinen, frames the west terrace of Marquis Hall. Inverted three-stage fluted capitals, a characteristic Saarinen motif, top the four stone piers. By the staircase that descends from the terrace of Marquis Hall to the quadrangle by the Dining Hall entrance, *The Running Dogs (Coursing Hounds)* sculpture by Carl Milles seems to be racing furiously into the quadrangle, the dogs jostling each other as they go. The dogs are the hounds of Diana, goddess of the hunt. Milles made them at Lidingo, Sweden, at the request of Lord Melchett of England.

Page Hall memorializes the Right Reverend Herman Page, bishop of the Protestant Episcopal Diocese of Michigan from 1924 to 1940. It contains Page Hall Common (Upper School Common Room), a spacious room that served originally as a recreation room and lounge for the boys of the Upper School. Here social assemblies and informal afternoon dances were held.

Stevens Terrace connects Stevens Hall with Page Hall. Stevens Hall (Senior Dormitory) was named for William Oliver Stevens, the first headmaster of Cranbrook School from 1927–1935. A pergola topped with an exquisite nine-foot-square wrought-iron dome by Eliel Saarinen marks the entry to the terrace.

The Gateway of Friendship (Friendship Arch), located between Stevens Hall and the Master's Club, gives access from the north to the Cranbrook School Quadrangle. Carved in stone beneath the center arch are the words, "Gateway of Friendship," and above and on both sides of the arches are the quotations of philosophers: "True friendship can only subsist between those who are animated by the strictest principles of honor and virtue" (Cicero); "It is a good thing to be rich and a good thing to be strong, but it is a better thing to be beloved of

Metalwork Dome/Pergola, West Terrace, Page Hall, Cranbrook School

many friends" (Euripides); "Friendship that flows from the heart cannot be frozen by adversity as the water that flows from the spring cannot congeal in winter" (Cooper); "Be slow to fall into friendship, but when thou art in, continue firm and constant" (Socrates). At the opening of each new school year, students traditionally scrub the plaque inscribed Gateway of Friendship clean with soap and water, and people refrain from walking on it.

25. Dining Hall *Eliel Saarinen, 1928–1929*

Oolitic limestone trim from Bedford, Indiana, selected for its coarse formation, highlights the orange-reddish brown brick walls of the gabled dining
hall. For a brief time before this dining hall opened, a temporary kitchen
and dining hall was set up in a large farm storage building on the site of the
present Stevens Terrace. Initially the faculty and their families ate together
with the boys at assigned tables in the great barrel-vaulted dining hall. The
headmaster presided over the dining room from his seat at the head table,
and a master and his wife or an unmarried master headed up a table of
twelve or eight, respectively. After the headmaster said grace, the diners
sat down and were served by waiters. Following dinner, coffee was served
to faculty families and seniors in the Common Room of Page Hall or in
the lower auxiliary refectory beneath this room. This dining area is decorated with historical scenes and amusing school episodes painted by
Katherine McEwen. Beginning in the 1960s, dining became increasingly
informal. Today, casually dressed students from Cranbrook Kingswood
School and others help themselves to a cafeteria selection of fare prepared by commercial caterers, sit wherever they like, and return their own
trays to the kitchen.

A magnificent window of leaded glass in a geometric pattern on
the west wall and multiple pairs of leaded glass windows in the north and
south walls filter light to the room by day. Gorgeous Swedish Arts and
Crafts light fixtures, with amber glass globes, light it by night.

The *Clock of the Handicrafts*, 1927, hangs high on the east wall over
the fireplace. Quite pleased with metalsmith Oscar Bruno Bach's scheme to
depict the crafts in the bronze and
black wrought-iron dial of the clock,
Booth first considered placing the time
piece on the tower of the boys school.
Instead he put it on the east wall at the
end of the dining room, where "its size
and quality will fully count." Peacock
andirons were designed for the fireplace by Eliel Saarinen and fabricated
at Cranbrook by John C. Burnett.
Saarinen designed the furniture,
dishes and silverware. His son, Eero
Saarinen, designed the cranes inserted
in the backs of the arm and side chairs.

Clock of the Handicrafts *by Oscar Bach,*
Dining Hall, Cranbrook School

Rembrandt Peale's *Portrait of George Washington* once hung in the
foyer, but today is in the Page Hall Common.

Dining Hall, Cranbrook School

Infirmary, looking toward Marquis Arch, Cranbrook School

26. Infirmary   *Eliel Saarinen, 1927*

The little infirmary has a friendly domestic quality. South-facing upper windows of the two-story bay admitted sunlight to the room for convalescents. The building has living quarters for resident nurses. Before the infirmery opened, Tour Cottage at Cranbrook House served as the school's infirmary.

There are two wrought-iron gates opposite each other along the sidewalk leading to the academy. Another is at the Lone Pine entrance to the infirmary. All three were designed by Eero Saarinen, Eliel's son, and made by John C. Burnett. The gate to the court between the kitchen and infirmary is ornamented with a fantastical gracefully leaping hoofed animal crafted in wrought iron. The dining hall kitchen also connects to the infirmary.

27. James C. Gordon Hall of Science
Tarapata MacMahon Paulsen, 1975–1976

Gordon Hall, the Music Building, and the entrance corridor to Keppel Gymnasium fit together like pieces of a jigsaw puzzle. Together with Lerchen Hall, formerly the Little Gym, they wrap themselves around a small terraced court. Gordon Hall of Science was created from a remodeling and enlargement of Lindquist Hall, which had been designed by the Cranbrook Architectural Office and built in 1941. The main hall of the long, narrow rectangular building is oriented to a southern exposure. Light is admitted by a glass curtain wall and a clerestory. Laboratories and classrooms open two

James C. Gordon Hall of Science, Cranbrook School

abreast off the corridor. The little bronze *Robert E. Lee Group* (*Teachers of Youth*) sculpture by Carl Milles, depicting the Civil War general with an African-American and a Euro-American student, stands in the corridor.

28. Music Building (Music Studios)   *Eliel Saarinen, 1937*

The Music Building contains practice rooms and space for group rehearsals, private practice, and lessons.

29. Faculty Way Houses (formerly Faculty Row or Sunset Terrace Houses)   *Cranbrook Architectural Office, 1928–1930*

This row of two-story, hipped-roof single and multiple family faculty houses overlooks the River Rouge and the Cranbrook playing fields to the northwest. They are built of concrete block trimmed with red brick and have steel-sash casement windows. Some of the boxy houses are free standing; others share a common wall or are linked by connectors.

Faculty Way Houses

Valley Way Houses

30. Valley Way Houses (formerly Valley Farm Road Houses) *Cranbrook Architectural Office, 1929–1930*

Farm buildings, a laundry house, a dwelling, stable, and pump house originally occupied this valley that borders on the Cranbrook playing field to the
south. The Cranbrook Architectural Office built the Valley Way houses during the Depression as living quarters for the grounds and maintenance
workers and their families. The row of modest one-and-a-half story Cape
Cod and Colonial Revival cottages includes double houses, row cottages,
and single cottages. Mike Vettraino, superintendent of grounds, and his wife
and six children once occupied the large house on the north side of the road
at 24 Valley Way. In May 1933 the Faculty Way and Valley Way houses were
transferred to Cranbrook School. Despite recent sheathing with aluminum
siding, the Valley Way houses retain their original forms and relationship to
each other. Today most cottages house Cranbrook faculty and staff. The residents continue to work gardens that served as victory gardens during
World War II. Other buildings function as offices, workshops, and garages
for public safety, security, and maintenance.

31. Cranbrook Boys' Middle School Campus (formerly Bloomfield Hills School and Vaughan School) *J. Robert F. Swanson, 1932; additions, 1939, 1949–1950*

With its brick walls, slate roof, and bay window this neo-Tudor school building has a residential quality appropriate to its neighborhood. George Gough Booth acquired the land, first belonging to Peter A. Vaughan, in 1925, and donated it to the school district in 1931. The two-story building was completed in 1932, contained six classrooms, an office, and an auditorium. In 1939 two more classrooms and a library were added, followed—in 1949–1950—by an elementary school and kindergarten.

When the high school for Bloomfield Hills School District #2 opened in 1955, Bloomfield Hills School on Vaughan Road became an elementary school. This school was officially renamed Vaughan School in honor of Peter A. Vaughan. Today Vaughan School serves as the Cranbrook Boys' Middle School campus. Its large classrooms, wide corridors, ample playground, and proximity to the Cranbrook Campus work well for this purpose.

Cranbrook Boys' Middle School Campus

Cranbrook Academy of Art

32 | Art Academy/Administration Building

33 | Arts and Crafts Building and Dormitory and
Studios Addition

34 | Saarinen House (Group Residence # 1)

35 | Milles House (Group Residence # 2) and
Studio # 3

36 | Milles Studio (Studio # 4)

37 | Headmaster's Residence (Group Residence # 3)

38 | Academy Way Houses and Studios

39 | *Jonah and the Whale* and Lake Jonah

40 | Nichols Gate

41 | Cranbrook Academy of Art Museum and
Library and De Salle Auditorium

42 | Studio Addition

43 | Triton Pool Court

44 | Academy Quadrangle of the Museum
and Library

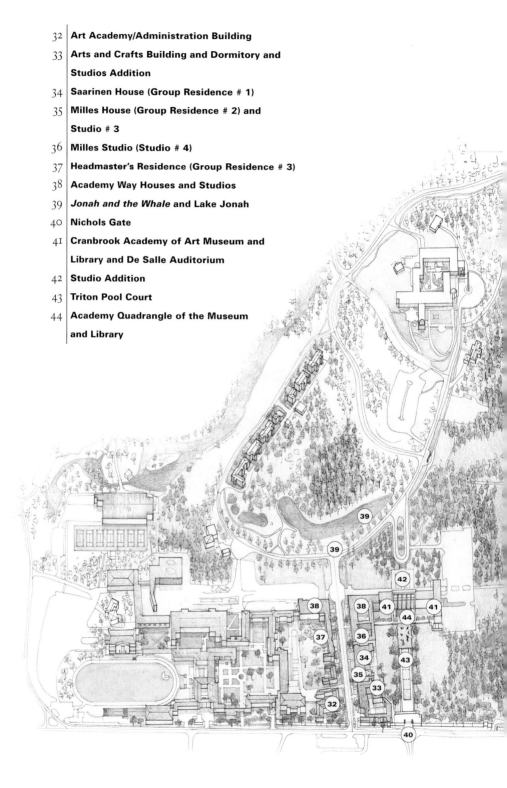

Designed as a place where teachers and students can work and live together, the Cranbrook Academy of Art is a group of utilitarian brick buildings with studios and living quarters that flank Academy Way. Entered from Lone Pine Road, this street forms the very spine of the academy. The faculty houses, both row and double houses with attached studios, and the dormitories are set behind a three-foot-high brick wall. Together they define courts and plazas, many of which face the broad garden area on the east. The main ceremonial entrance to the art academy is through the [Walter] Nichols Gate off Lone Pine Road. The whole is planned with courtyards and placed in an evocative landscape oriented around pools and sculpture.

     The academy is arranged with an east/west axis and two cross axes: the east/west axis runs from the West Terrace of Cranbrook House, up the Ramp of the Sacred Lion Dog, to the north quadrangle of the library and museum, then west to Williams Natatorium; one north/south axis runs from the estate's highest point at Sunset Hill through the propylaeum connecting the library and museum, south by stairs, terraces, and pools, then through the *Europa and the Bull* sculpture and Triton Pool to the Nichols Gate; another north/south axis extends from the automobile entrance off Lone Pine Road north up Academy Way to the *Jonah and the Whale* fountain sculpture and Lake Jonah. A studio addition to the museum designed by renowned museum architect Rafael Moneo of Madrid is under construction as this book goes to press.

     George Gough Booth attributed the origins of his idea to establish a community where artists could live and work in Bloomfield Hills to his visit to the American Academy in Rome in 1922. "The American Academy at Rome seemed to me to be a great contribution to the American Arts and Artists, and first suggested to me the idea of an Academy of Arts suited to the home land." The academy that Booth envisioned at Cranbrook was based on architecture, complemented by the full constellation of allied and applied arts: painting, sculpture, decoration, and landscape design. The consummate development of the academy would include musical composition, drama, horticulture, and all the fine and applied arts. The school would ultimately accommodate two hundred pupils. Booth believed, as he wrote in his notes in 1924, "that the number should be generous as this country is only just entering upon an era of world competition in the field of industrial arts and will soon have great need of trained talent in the pursuit of this endeavor as well as in the general pursuit of happiness born of true culture." A community where artists could live and work is an embodiment of the Arts and Crafts movement. Contemporary journalist Martin Filler measured Booth's vision in a 1982 *House and Garden* article: "In the Midwestern American tradition of philanthropic civic responsibility, Booth envisioned a school like no other in this country: an academy that stressed the inseparability of art and craft, science and technology, housed in a setting of great beauty planned to instill high artistic values through inspiring example."

Active in the Art Alliance of America and the American Federation of Arts, Booth saw the need for good design in Detroit, where the automobile manufacturing industries were burgeoning. He had participated in the establishment of the Detroit Society of Arts and Crafts in 1906 and was instrumental in the society's founding of the Detroit School of Design in 1911. When the latter closed for economic reasons in 1918, Booth nurtured the formation of the Art School of the Detroit Society of Arts and Crafts, which survives today as the Center for Creative Studies (See Walk Nine). He was active in the development of the architecture program at the University of Michigan in Ann Arbor, where his son, Henry Scripps Booth, was a student from 1918 through 1924. Booth supported the efforts of Emil Lorch, the first head and organizer of the department of architecture in the College of Engineering, to establish a separate and autonomous college of architecture and design, and to design and build a four-story building for the college in 1925–1927. Booth also established the Booth travel fellowship for university students.

Henry Scripps Booth developed a series of drawings for his father's proposed art academy as part of his thesis at the University of Michigan in 1924. Upon his graduation in 1924, the younger Booth and his classmate J. Robert F. Swanson opened the architectural practice of Swanson and Booth in the Italian Cottage, later the site of Hedgegate, north of Brookside School. The firm's first architectural projects were the design of Thornlea, several houses in a subdivision just south of Cranbrook, as well as the Cranbrook Architectural Office and the early schematic work on Cranbrook School.

As early as 1924 Eliel Saarinen developed a plan with sketches for the art academy that was based somewhat on Henry Booth's suggested plan—that is, on an axis with the West Terrace of Cranbrook House and Gardens. The younger Booth had planned the northern courtyards of the proposed academy on an east/west axis along the length of the West Terrace of the gardens of Cranbrook House. Saarinen retained this scheme in the final plans as the *Ramp of the Sacred Lion Dog* and the walkway along the north side of the academy museum and library. Today this axis continues west, terminating in the Williams Natatorium. In preliminary correspondence with Saarinen, Booth permitted the architect great flexibility, writing him in 1924 that "if you have a somewhat different vision I hope you will not hesitate to feel that the whole territory is open for you to consider." Booth encouraged Saarinen to spend a day with him at Cranbrook with a topographical map in hand so as to fit his plan to land's contours.

Henry Scripps Booth, J. Robert F. Swanson, Emil Lorch, and Albert Kahn had touted Eliel Saarinen's abilities, and by 1925 George Gough

Booth was independently seeking Saarinen's counsel. In 1925 the elder Booth asked Saarinen, then a visiting professor of architecture at the University of Michigan, having been recruited by Emil Lorch, to prepare a master plan for the art academy at Cranbrook and to offer advice on its educational philosophy. Booth said, "I am having prepared by Mr. Eliel Saarinen an idealistic plan, based on an accurate survey that a greater hope may be stimulated and that each step in the way of building or ground improvement may be working towards this ultimate goal which others must carry to completion."

Twenty-five years later, in the essay "The Story of Cranbrook," Saarinen recalled that Booth, in the spring of 1925, told him:

> I happen to have two things: first, I happen to have money, and second, I happen to have a great interest in art. And my profound desire is to use my money to the good of the people so as to further and broaden interest, understanding and appreciation of good art.
>
> Now, as I have been weighing the matter in my mind, there might be three different ways to approach this matter. First, I could collect works of the great masters of the past—which I have already done [to] a certain degree—but, I am afraid, this probably would help only the art-dealer's pocket-book. Second, I would order works of art from living artists—which I have already done to a certain degree—but I do not know always what I get, and my experience in this hasn't always been very encouraging. Now, however, I might have a third course to take, and just about this course I [would] like to have your advice.
>
> Supposing now that I would found somewhere on the Cranbrook grounds or elsewhere, if this will better further my ideas, an Academy of Art where artists of high standing . . . would live and execute their art work. Undoubtedly this would create a healthy atmosphere of art education about the place. Supposing, furthermore, that I would undertake such steps—as, for example, the gradual development of basic schools of various kinds—which would be apt to bring young people of various ages to live about these Academy grounds, with their atmosphere of art creation. Don't you think the young minds would be inclined to seek such inspiration from such an active art environment, particularly if they would be given the opportunity to do this during the course of several years?"

Saarinen was an exponent of the Arts and Crafts movement and the Vienna secessionists, who rebelled against the salon system that flourished at the turn of the century. For him architecture was *gesamtkunstwerke*, that is, it encompassed all aspects of design. Together, in 1925, Saarinen and Booth began preparing a visionary plan for the academy.

Booth concluded that Cranbrook would be devoted to the art academy, less portions of the campus that would be set aside for boys', girls', and children's schools, and less the life use of Cranbrook House and Gardens. One-hundred-seventy-five acres would be designated for the art academy. The elevated site on Sunset Hill was bounded by Lone Pine Road on the south and Cranbrook School on the west.

Before moving from Ann Arbor to Bloomfield Hills, Saarinen created a grand study for the academy that rolled over Cranbrook's western terrain. Comprising courtyards, studios, dormitories, offices, lecture halls, towers, greenhouses, formal gardens, and pools, the plan was appealing but too ambitious for Booth. The view would be eastward to Cranbrook House. A formal garden axis north from Lone Pine Road would lead to a linked pair of monumental buildings, later realized as the library and museum. Residences and academy buildings would flank Academy Way. Loja Saarinen, Eliel's wife, produced a scale model of the plan her husband designed, but, after the academy had been built, Booth had it destroyed for fear that people would think that he had begun something he could not finish. As executed, no buildings at the art academy were built north and east of the library and museum.

In the fall of 1925 Saarinen moved to Bloomfield Hills, mostly focusing his energy on consulting on plans for the Cranbrook Architectural Office and Cranbrook boys' school. Yet he also continued to interpret in conceptual plans Booth's vision for the art academy.

To run the academy, Booth contemplated in 1925 that a general trust might be created to hold the money or other securities upon which the initial project would be based and a directorate of some fifteen specialists organized to help to ensure the growth and success of the project. Chosen at the outset would be one or two talented and experienced leaders to take the active work in hand. Only gifted, well-educated young men would be admitted to the academy, and admitted free, including board, for a post-graduate course of two years or more. At the conclusion of their work and study at the academy, a "fellowship" providing for one year of travel and study in Europe would be available. It was anticipated that successful graduates would feel honor bound to help others in their academy work by a sojourn and service of some reasonable period at the academy without compensation. Faculty would undertake suitable professional work on their own account, not interfering with their obligations to the academy, in the development of which work the student body might assist or otherwise benefit. As to the architecture, all permanent buildings at the academy would be examples of good design and the right use of materials.

On September 10, 1927, the Cranbrook Academy of Art was outlined as an educational entity, and on November 28, 1927, the seven trustees signed the document establishing the Cranbrook Foundation: George Gough Booth, Gustavus D. Pope, Henry Schoolcraft Hulbert, Samuel Simpson Marquis, and Booth's sons Warren Scripps Booth, James Scripps Booth, and Henry Scripps Booth.

By November 1927, at the urging of architect Henry Booth and his partner Swanson, George Booth formalized Saarinen's involvement with the academy and the boys' school projects. Saarinen was named chief architectural officer in charge of most new building projects for Cranbrook. For his services he received one thousand dollars per month, one half of which was paid by the Cranbrook Architectural Office and one half by the Cranbrook Foundation.

The development of the academy's educational philosophy proceeded slowly. The Arts and Crafts Department, the studios of which opened in 1928–1929, was, in fact, the actual precursor to the Cranbrook Academy of Art as it is known today. The group of artists and craftsmen, mostly European friends and colleagues of Saarinen, who were assembled at Cranbrook to design, enhance, and embellish the buildings and grounds of the various institutions then under construction or recently completed—Christ Church Cranbrook (1925–1928), Cranbrook School (1926–1928), the ongoing additions to Brookside School (1923 to the 1930s), and, later, Kingswood School (1930–1931)—ran these studios and formed the real nucleus of an academy. While this work was in progress a few students were accepted as apprentices to the architects and artists, and it was from this beginning that in 1932 the academy was organized as a division of the foundation.

Geza Maroti, architect, sculptor and painter, arrived from Budapest, Hungary, in January 1927 to embellish Cranbrook with his decorative sculpture. Arthur Nevill Kirk, the English silversmith, came in the fall of 1927 to work on ceremonial objects for Christ Church Cranbrook and to organize the metalsmith shop. Henry P. Macomber, former director of the Boston Society of Arts and Crafts, came in October 1928 to coordinate the craft activity. At this time a few students were admitted as apprentices to the architects, artists, and craftsmen. Thus, with the founding of the numerous craft studios for printing, bookbinding, silver-work, weaving, cabinet-work and ceramics, the first component of the academy—the advanced art school—was established. The first academy students arrived in November 1930. Resident artists were selected to live and work with advanced creative students, who executed their own work under the leadership of the masters. Within this atelier setting the individual's artistic identity developed.

By 1931, also in studios in the Arts and Crafts Building, Loja Gesellius Saarinen, an accomplished weaver and textile designer, oversaw the Textile and Weaving Department; Jean Eschmann, the Book Bindery Department; Tor Berglund, the Cabinet Shop; and Eva Lisa (Pipsan) Saarinen Swanson, daughter of Eliel and Loja Saarinen, the Batik Department. Carl Milles, the great Swedish-born European sculptor, arrived at Cranbrook in 1931 to serve as a guest artist, working on projects for the foundation and heading the Sculpture Department. Later, others would join

Loja Saarinen and Maja Andersson-Wirde in Studio Loja, Cranbrook Academy of Art, Cranbrook Archives

the faculty and by 1938 the following were employed in the studios: William Comstock, instructor of design; Marshall M. Fredericks, instructor of modeling; Wallace Mitchell, instructor of painting and drawing; Marianne Strengell, Finnish-born instructor of weaving and costume design; Maija Grotell, Finnish-born instructor of ceramics; and Harry Bertoia, Italianborn, Detroit-educated, metal craftsman.

The second component of the academy was the Intermediate Art School. It provided possibilities for a younger group of students to study at the academy. Although the organizers had hoped to enroll students from the boys' school, as it evolved, students were drawn from outside the Cranbrook institutions. But in this spirit of a dual institution—the advanced and the intermediate—the academy functioned for many years as an art school for creative artists.

In 1932, at Booth's urging, the Cranbrook Foundation authorized the establishment of the Cranbrook Academy of Art, offering the first presidency of the academy of art to Eliel Saarinen. He assumed responsibility for the entire art program, including the crafts, the art library, and the art museum, and served in this post until 1946. At that time the programs of the academy operated in the Arts and Crafts Building; the library, museum, and the painting and etching classes were housed in the Art Academy Building; and students and faculty boarded in the Art Club Building.

The character and mode of the Cranbrook Academy of Art is set forth in the donors' deed, a document that states that the academy of art "will afford talented and highly trained students the opportunity of pursuing their studies in a favorable environment and under the leadership of artists and architects of high repute." Two fundamental principles guided the academy. First, the academy was a center of creation where artists of the various branches could live and work, and where talented art students were given the opportunity to execute their own work under the leadership of these artists. Second, the academy embraced a flexible educational policy to meet changing conditions and demands. According to Saarinen, the primary function of the academy was "to understand the spirit of our time" and "to create an adequate form to express this spirit." Parallel with the academy a School of Arts and Crafts operated.

Crafts shops were individual enterprises in which individual work was executed. Their life depended on finding a market for art. Although the Cranbrook Academy of Art could not undertake this activity because of its status as an educational institution with cultural aims, the crafts shops as private enterprises could. The craftsmen could also work at Cranbrook School, the Art School of the Detroit Society of Arts and Crafts, and later, at Kingswood, and they could offer classes for the public. In 1933, after the opening of the academy and after the full effect of the Depression had been felt, the shops closed because of lack of funds.

Saarinen and Booth attributed the success of the academy to the fundamental doctrine-free principles conveyed to the students and to the quality of art work done by the instructors and students in the workshops and studios. The academy's accomplishments were manifest in many exhibitions, in the national reputation of the faculty and graduates, and in the prizes they were awarded.

By 1942 there was a need for the more practical orientation toward the development of a graduate school for professionals in industrial design, architectural design, and art education. With the opening of its new museum and library in May 1942, the academy became an educational, policy-making, and administrative unit separate from the foundation. It was set up as a separate non-profit trustee institution of higher learning incorporated under the educational laws of Michigan and authorized to grant degrees. Today the academy continues to offer the Master of Fine Arts and the Master of Architecture degrees. The art museum was intended to house artworks acquired from the George Gough Booth collection through the Cranbrook Foundation, and, as a teaching institution, its permanent collections and exhibitions serve as a teaching tool for the academy.

World War II intervened, but in the 1940s art academy members shaped modern design in America. *Design in America: The Cranbrook Vision 1925–1950*, an exhibition at the Detroit Institute of Arts and the Metropolitan

Museum of Art in 1983–1985, documented the role of Cranbrook artists in the emergence of modern American design at that time. It celebrated the achievements and influences of such great Cranbrook artists as Charles Eames, Harry Bertoia, Florence Knoll, and Eero Saarinen.

Today the graduate studies catalog of the Cranbrook Academy of Art stresses that the academy remains a "living studio of artistic invention" with departments in architecture, ceramics, design, fiber, metalsmithing, painting, photography, printmaking, and sculpture. It is a community of artists and students and an internationally recognized school of art, design, and architecture. Here 150 graduate students study for two years with distinguished practicing artists. The academy imposes "no dogma or artistic constraints" and nurtures "individual innovation and personal growth."

The exalted purpose of the academy remains one of assisting in satisfying mankind's aesthetic, social, and spiritual needs through education in the arts. In *Precepts Governing Cranbrook* (1934–1935) Eliel Saarinen said that Cranbrook Academy of Art is not an art school in the ordinary meaning. Rather "it is a working place for creative art." Its purpose is to bring understanding of the underlying principles of art, of its forms and design, so that the student will develop a true and expressive 'Art of our Time'—and of no other time.

32. Art Academy/Administration Building (formerly Cranbrook Architectural Office)

Swanson and Booth with Eliel Saarinen as advisor, 1925–1926

The Art Academy/Administration Building was the first building erected in the art academy group, and, like other early buildings at the art academy, its contemporized medieval vocabulary executed in imported Dutch brick resembles the buildings constructed at Cranbrook School.

The main section of the L-shaped original building is perpendicular to Lone Pine Road, with a wing extending eastward from its north end. The draftsmen of the Cranbrook Architectural Office occupied the primary downstairs rooms, and Geza Maroti had his design and sculpture studio in the skylighted space upstairs. The lower level of the wing was intended for use as a garage and was built at ground level without a basement. But the space was urgently needed for the Cranbrook Architectural Office, which opened shop as an independent architectural firm in 1926 in this building. The office was a beehive of activity with designers, many of whom were former University of Michigan students, preparing drawings and specifications in consultation with Eliel Saarinen for all the building projects then underway for the Cranbrook institutions. (From 1926 to 1930, as the design and building activity on the boys' and girls' schools escalated, the staff of

Art Academy Building/Administration Building, Cranbrook Academy of Art

the Cranbrook Architectural Office rose to some twenty-four.) So windows were quickly installed in the archways that had been intended for garage doors, and the space was finished inside for this purpose. Booth's offices and those of the Cranbrook Foundation occupied the first floor of the north/south wing, and the second floor was converted into the art library.

In 1929, a wing was added to the north of the original building, containing a room with ample light for studio use; a basement was excavated under the original east and west wing.

The building has served as office space for the art academy; temporary display rooms for the art collection; and students' painting studios, woodworking shop, and print shop. Later, in 1942, when the art library moved to its new quarters, this space was used by the foundation, but their offices were moved to the headmaster's residence north of this building.

The sculpture of a mermaid or water nymph grasping a large succulent golden fish, *Siren with Fishes*, rests in a fountain west of Academy Way on the path between the Academy/Administration Building and the headmaster's house, leading to the Cranbrook School campus. Carl Milles gave the sculpture to the foundation and installed it in the summer of 1935.

Siren with Fishes *sculpture by Carl Milles, Art Academy and Administration Building, Cranbrook Academy of Art*

33. Arts and Crafts Building and Dormitory and Studios Addition *Eliel Saarinen, 1928–1929*

Along the border of Lone Pine Road east of Academy Way is the Arts and Crafts Building and the Dormitory (formerly the Art Club), dining room and kitchen, the ceramic and sculpture, weaving, silver, cabinet-work, and the architecture design studios. Together they embrace a little crafts court dedicated to ceramist Maija Grotell and so identified by two ceramic wall plaques. Access to the Maija Grotell Court, formerly the Crafts Court, from the formal gardens to the east is by way of stairs that divide in pairs until they reach a landing west of the archway. One's ascent is pleasantly interrupted by views of sculptures by Carl Milles: A *Pair of Running Deer* (circa 1925) marks the upper landing to the east of the archway.

In the beginning there were five crafts shops in the Arts and Crafts Building operated independently as enterprises by the craftsmen: Printing, Edward A. Miller; Binding, Jean Eschmann; Cabinet Shop, Tor Berglund; Silversmithing, Arthur Neville Kirk; and Weaving, Loja Saarinen. One year later a kiln was installed. Waylande DeSantis Gregory was the ceramic sculptor. Silversmithing, ceramics, and weaving studios survived as departments of the Cranbrook Academy of Art.

The studio Loja Saarinen occupied in the southwest corner of the building now serves as a metalworking studio for the artist-in-residence. Evidence of her occupancy as head of the weaving department is seen by the paintings by her daughter, Pipsan Saarinen Swanson, above the fireplace on the north wall, on the storage cupboards, and on the beamed ceiling decorated with six textile-related scenes, including shearing the ram for wool, and growing cotton.

Maija Grotell Court, Arts and Crafts Building, Cranbrook Academy of Art

34. Saarinen House (Eliel and Louise Gesellius Saarinen House /Academy Group Residence # 1)

Eliel Saarinen, 1929–1930

When the Saarinens first came from Ann Arbor to Cranbrook in 1925, they lived in one of the original 1911 farmhouses that had been designed by Burrowes and Wells on the site of Cranbrook School. That concrete block house, altered in 1924 to serve as a single house for gardeners and laborers, was converted into a double house a year later to also include the Saarinens. However, noise and activity from the construction at the new school was bothersome, so the Saarinens moved into a studio apartment at Towerknoll, the new home of their daughter and son-in-law, Pipsan and J. Robert Swanson at 955 Lone Pine Road (at the southeast corner Lahser Road, see Walk Eight). Here they stayed until their own house on Academy Way was completed in 1930.

In November 1928, only months after the board of trustees of the Cranbrook Foundation authorized the building of houses for the Saarinens and for Geza Maroti—the Hungarian sculptor who was enhancing the boys' school with his decorative sculpture—Saarinen completed plans for the double house. Albert Wermuth of Charles R. Wermuth and Son, had construction underway in 1929. The Saarinen house was ready for occupancy in September 1930, as the Saarinens returned from their annual summer in Finland. Carl Milles replaced Maroti as sculptor at Cranbrook, and the Milleses moved into Residence # 2 in 1931. The

Saarinen House, Academy Way, Cranbrook Academy of Art

Living Room, Saarinen House, Cranbrook Academy of Art

Saarinens lived in their house until Eliel Saarinen died in 1950. Then Loja
Saarinen moved to a small studio house on Vaughan Road behind Eero
Saarinen's Italianate house (See Walk Eight). Saarinen House underwent
a full museum-quality restoration that was completed in 1994. The history
of the house and the remarkable restoration process is fully chronicled in
Gregory Wittkopp's book, *Saarinen House and Garden: A Total Work of
Art* (1995).

Reddish brown brick made in Ohio defines the exterior of this austere double house. The hipped roof clad with green clay tiles and manufactured by Ludowici Celadon of Chicago resembles slate. The wings contain a
studio in one and loggia in the other, each of which borders a courtyard
extending to the east. The courtyard is paved with flagstones radiating from
the centrally placed bronze nymph statue, *Kivi's Muse*, of 1926, by Finnish
artist Vaino Aaltonen.

Saarinen House was planned to accommodate both the private life
of a reserved couple and the public life of the leading academy family
engaged in creative artistic work with students, faculty, and the administration. Here individual or group conferences and annual academy tea parties
took place as well as small cocktail parties and dinners for friends, colleagues, and visitors. The Saarinens arranged the social, domestic, and private spaces to be open and flexible, yet well-defined and tucked in
comfortable alcoves throughout. The hallway that runs nearly the full front

of Saarinen House (as well as Milles House and the other residences on Academy Way) shields the main part of the house from the street.

At Saarinen House, the axis of the living and dining rooms begins at the center of the dining room table and runs dramatically the full length of the living room. It focuses on the fireplace faced with brown and silver ceramic tile by Mary Chase Perry Stratton at the Pewabic Pottery in Detroit and accented with bronze peacock andirons. Perpendicular to this axis is the cross axis that begins with the Greta Skogster wall tapestry depicting a landscape and runs through the center of the dining room to the courtyard and Triton Pool and woods beyond. Portieres could be drawn closed between the dining room, living room, and the studio, affording privacy to activities and conversations in any area.

The glorious golden dining room was the place where the Saarinens entertained. The octagonal room perfectly accommodates its round table. The walls are lined with natural fir panels, and the interiors of the corner niches are painted Chinese red. A central stepped and gilded domed ceiling diffuses the reflected light, and from its center is hung a round brass light fixture with indirect light. The furnishings for the dining room and the living room are considered among the finest and most famous Art Deco furniture produced in America. The table was constructed to reveal contrasting grains in an octagonal pattern, and the fluted-backed chairs are of fir painted with black in imitation of ebony inlay. Designed by Eliel Saarinen, they were manufactured by the Company of Master Craftsmen, a division of W. and J. Sloane in New York. The dining room and its furnishings, and the table linens, silver and brass flatware and hollow ware, the dishes, and even the food itself (pineapple upside down cake), presented a total work of art. Eliel Saarinen explained, "Art is an expression of life. . . . It is not in the monumental buildings, but in the home, in the living and working place, and in man's contact with even the smallest objects he uses and lives with."

The alcove or ante-room to the barrel-vaulted studio, which is connected by covered walkway to the studio of the architecture department, was the cozy corner of the house most frequently used by the Saarinens for conversations with each other and with students, clients, and grandchildren. Here the wall is fitted with leaded-glass windows. A built-in bench draped with a *ryijy* rug in jade and gray designed by Loja Saarinen wraps around two sides of the alcove.

Hand-woven wall hangings, textiles and rugs, and upholstery designed by Loja Saarinen and furniture designed by Eliel Saarinen and handcrafted in the cabinetry studio of Tor Berglund, silverware and light fixtures created by Saarinen and made in the craft studios fill and enhance Saarinen House.

Dining Room, Saarinen House, Cranbrook Academy of Art

In its spatial flow along interior axes, the open studio space, the ornamentation, and the communal proximity to the academy houses and studios, Saarinen House recalls Hvittrask, Saarinen's romantic but functional country home and studio near Helsinki. Situated on the crest of a thickly wooded hill overlooking Hvittrask or White Lake, Saarinen and his partners—Herman Gesellius and Armas Lindgren—built Hvittrask in 1902 as a refuge from the distractions of the city for themselves, their families, and assistants. (Their friends included the composers Jean Sibelius and Gustav Mahler, and the writer Maxim Gorky.) Hvittrask, blending Finnish romanticism with elements from the Arts and Crafts movement and art nouveau, displays the Finnish national spirit. Its rock foundation, dark shingles and red tiles seem to grow out of the wooded cliff, logs line the walls of the great hall, and massive beams support its high wooden ceiling. Saarinen's wooden furniture shows the influence of William Morris's Arts and Crafts designs.

Master Bath, Saarinen House, Cranbrook Academy of Art

35. Milles House (Carl Emil Anderson and Olga Granner Milles House/Academy Group Residence # 2) and Studio # 3

Milles House *Eliel Saarinen, 1929–1930*
Studio # 3 *Eliel Saarinen, 1930*

Toothpick sculpture, Milles House, Cranbrook Academy of Art

Carl Emil Anderson and Olga Granner Milles lived in this house from 1931 to 1951, during the twenty years that the sculptor worked at Cranbrook. This house and the adjacent sculpture studio were part of the inducement George Gough Booth offered Milles on behalf of the Cranbrook Foundation to entice him to come to Cranbrook. Booth also gave the artist a limited teaching schedule so that he would have ample time in his studio. Booth agreed to purchase sixty-three pieces of his work for some $120,000. Today Cranbrook owns seventy Milles sculptures, making the Cranbrook holdings the largest collection of Milles's work outside Sweden. Carl Milles created his very first work for Cranbrook—the *Jonah and the Whale* fountain—in this studio. Later, Milles's personal collection of antique Greek and Roman sculpture filled the main room, studio, and garden court of his house.

36. Milles Studio (Academy Studio # 4)

Eliel Saarinen, 1931-1932; Robert H. Snyder, alterations, 1956

To give Milles sufficient space in which to sculpt the huge onyx *Peace Memorial* under commission for installation in the Saint Paul City Hall, Booth authorized the construction of this thirty-foot-high studio. Later, in 1956, the studio space was altered.

37. Headmaster's House (Academy Group Residence # 3)

Eliel Saarinen, 1928–1929; Henry Scripps Booth, alterations, 1946

Constructed as a residence for the headmaster of Cranbrook School, the house is located on Academy Way, north of the Administration Building. Its first use was as office space for the Cranbrook Foundation, when the growth of the art academy crowded it out of the Administration Building. A portion of the building was also used at that time as an apartment for Palmer Black, one of the maintenance men. The availability of the house for these purposes was due to the preference of William O. Stevens, headmaster at the time, to remain in residence in the Pickell house, later the Orchard Ridge Apartments, on Orchard Ridge Road; he wished to live slightly removed from the boys' school. The second headmaster, Rudolph Lindquist, lived in the house. In 1942, the building was officially given to the Cranbrook Academy of Art.

38. Academy Way Houses and Studios

Academy Studio # 5   *Eliel Saarinen, 1932–1933*
Foundry   *Snyder and Wilson Associates, 1963*
Dormitory # 2   *Eliel Saarinen, 1936*
Studios (# 6 and 7) Addition,   *1939*
Residences # 3 to # 6   *Eliel Saarinen, 1938*
Academy of Art Ceramics Studios   *1941*
Academy Garage and Apartment   *Eliel Saarinen, 1938*

In drafting rooms and studios for architecture, sculpture, painting, life drawing, etching, and the like the academy helped students create an expressive art form in the spirit of our time. Cranbrook educators and practitioners believed that adequate design had to be developed in actual work with the best hands, in its real material, in many different fields, and in connection with the various needs of daily life.

The women's dormitory is located on the east side of Academy Way just north of Studio # 4 (Milles Studio). Studios # 6 and # 7 extend east from Dormitory # 2. The opening of the women's dormitory turned the formerly coed Art Club into a men's only dormitory. Located on the west side of Academy Way, north of the Headmaster's House, the academy residences (# 3 to # 6) comprise four two-story apartments or houses. The garage and apartment stands just north of Residences # 3, 4, 5, and 6.

39. *Jonah and the Whale* and Lake Jonah

Jonah and the Whale   *Carl Milles, sculptor, 1932*
Lake Jonah   *Cranbrook Architectural Office, 1933*

When he came to Cranbrook, Carl Milles was commissioned to create a fountain for the Academic Court at Kingswood School. He designed this plump Jonah sitting on the lower jaw of the whale as he is leaving the whale after a three-day submarine voyage within it. Too massive for its intended space in the Academic Court at Kingswood, the *Jonah and the Whale* sculpture was installed in 1933 at the end of Academy Way. As construction was underway, Milles decided he needed more water to support the whale visually, and with more water, he enthusiastically added more and more fish, until the fountain became too small to catch the spray. At Booth's suggestion the artist added a lower basin. Jonah of the *Jonah and the Whale* Fountain sculpture gave his name to the whale-shaped concrete-lined man-made lake behind it.

Jonah and the Whale *fountain by Carl Milles, Cranbrook Academy of Art*

Nichols Gate, Cranbrook Academy of Art

40. Nichols Gate   *Eliel Saarinen, 1941*

Walter Nichols, Cranbrook's resident blacksmith, fabricated this wrought-iron gate, the ceremonial entrance to the Cranbrook Academy of Art. A pair of sitting wild boars, another of Carl Milles's sculptures, dating from around 1926, overlooks Lone Pine Road seemingly awaiting the arrival of patrons.

41. Cranbrook Academy of Art Museum and Library and DeSalle Auditorium

Cranbrook Academy of Art Museum and Library   *Eliel Saarinen, 1938–1942*
Albert and Peggy De Salle Auditorium
>*Robert Saarinen Swanson with Jickling, Lyman and Powell and with George Zonars, interior architect, 1985–1986*

The most distinctive building in the academy and the focus of the formal garden axis from Nichols Gate to Orpheus Fountain is the monumental Cranbrook Academy of Art Museum and Library. The classical building reduced to simple terms appears to be two structures connected by a dramatic but quiet propylaeum, but, in reality, its foundations form a single unit.

The building was constructed to contain the collection of over six thousand books and the antique and modern art works that the Booths

Cranbrook Art Museum and Library (looking southeast), Cranbrook Academy of Art

had gathered together for the art academy, some of which had been housed in the Art Academy/Administration Building from the time the academy was established.

Saarinen's original plan called for a pair of small museums at the head of a terraced pool in the center of a broad formal garden. By 1940 the site had been graded, and the pools built. In the plan that was executed, the structures were narrowed, extended, and turned at the east end so as to face north and south, with the western unit designated for the art library. At the suggestion of James Scripps Booth, academy trustee and the founders' oldest child, who thought the joining of the two roofs and their support on piers would be monotonous, the roof was raised to create a distinct, separate roof for the propylaeum or monumental gateway to the buildings that is the terminus of the axis from Nichols Gate.

The large open propylaeum shelters the entrances to the museum and library and forms the central architectural feature of the building. It ties the building to the axis defined by the two terraced open spaces—the one on the north with the Orpheus Fountain, and the other on the south, an elongated formal garden with the *Europa and the Bull* sculpture and the Triton Pool stepping down in graduated terraces. This provides a spacious outdoor room of grand proportions from which to view the formal gardens with their rich display of powerful and heroic sculptures by Carl Milles and others. Pale orange-yellow Mankato limestone paves the floor of the porch and clads its walls and columns, and concrete, into which are incised lineal patterns, covers the ceiling. Mottled pale yellowish brown brick is laid in the exterior walls of the building above an exposed foundation of Mankato limestone.

Bronze museum doors are sculpted in a plastic linear manner that resembles carved wooden doors. The geometrically patterned bronze doors of the library entrance contrast with the large expanse of plain brick wall. The central pedestal supports a concealed lighting fixture.

The classic monumentality of the functional building is in the spirit of the Woodland Crematorium (1935–1940) by Erik Gunnar Asplund in Stockholm, Sweden.

The finely proportioned museum interior is arranged with galleries, storage vaults, staff offices, bookstore, and auditorium. Artificial lighting can be controlled accurately to give each item of the collection its own special conditions. General illumination is diffused from the grid and reflecting coffers above. Cases and blocks are portable to give complete flexibility in rearranging the exhibits. The floor is Roman travertine marble; walls are cloth covered plywood; ceilings are painted plaster. Colors are warm gray.

Entrance Doors, Library, Cranbrook Academy of Art

Gallery, Cranbrook Art Museum, Cranbrook Academy of Art

Folke Filblyter *sculpture by Carl Milles,*
Propylaeum, Cranbrook Art Museum and
Library, Cranbrook Academy of Art

On a pedestal in front of one of the stone columns on the southern side of the propylaeum stands *Folke Filblyter on a Horse*. This bronze sculpture, from around 1924 by Carl Milles, is a reduction of the central figure of the Folkunga fountain in Linkoping, Sweden.

The 200-seat De Salle Auditorium is housed in an underground wing of the art academy museum, which fills excavated space beneath the quadrangle. It was designed by Robert Swanson, grandson of Eliel Saarinen, to defer to the monumental museum and library. Underground additions to historic buildings quietly respect the historic building. In this way, Gunnar Birkerts, a former associate of Eero Saarinen and Alvar Aalto, designed an underground addition to the law library of the University of Michigan in 1977–1981, which enhanced the original Gothic beauty of the Law School Quadrangle and the pedestrian access to it.

42. Studio Addition   *Rafael Moneo, 2001*

Contemporary art has grown in scale, but the art academy studios have remained essentially unchanged for fifty years. This fact placed limitations on the art created in them. Needed were new studios for students with room for movement and freedom to create. The Studio Addition is one of the five construction projects detailed in the *Cranbrook Vision*.

The new studio building is designed as a three-story, L-shaped brick, metal, and glass addition connected to the south wing of the art museum. A three-story connector with galleries on all floors will join with sliding doors to the existing museum and to the new studios. From the connector the ell will extend to the east and to the north, creating a courtyard through which the entrance will be approached by way of a series of ramps and platforms. The new studios will house the departments of metalsmithing, ceramics, and fiber. Forty-eight studios are arranged on three floors with those turning out the heaviest work on the lowest level and those turning out the lightest products on the highest level. The artist-in-residence studios will be located in the angle of the ell on the floor appropriate to his or her area of work. At the north end of the ell will be the shop area.

Model (looking southeast), Studios Addition by Rafael Moneo, Cranbrook Art Museum, Cranbrook Academy of Art

The building will be arranged so that activities conducted within it are related horizontally by department and vertically by activity. Each department will have the use of the gallery space on its floor, and the connection of the studios with its gallery and the museum itself will express the worthiness of student work.

Exterior building materials will suggest the activities of the interior spaces. The north-facing glass curtain wall of the mid-section will reveal the studio area; metal exterior walls will tell of the industrial-like shop area, and the ventilating stacks of kilns rising above the roof will confirm this.

Born in Tudela, Navarra, Spain, in 1937, Jose Rafael Moneo studied at the Madrid School of Architecture, earning a Ph.D. in 1963, and was a fellow at the Spanish Academy in Rome from 1963–1965. He served as dean of the department of architecture at Harvard from 1985–1990, and currently he is a visiting professor at Harvard. Moneo's architectural practice is in Madrid, and most of his work has been done in Spain. This includes the Seville International Airport Terminal, the National Museum of Roman Art in Merida, and the Town Hall in Logrono. In the United States he designed the Davis Museum at Wellesley College and the Houston Museum of Art. He was awarded the Pritzker Architecture Prize in 1996.

The spacious, improved studios of this addition will enable the Cranbrook Academy of Art to maintain its national and international status as a premier graduate program in the visual arts.

Europa and the Bull *and* Triton *sculptures by Carl Milles, Triton Pool, Cranbrook Art Museum and Library, Cranbrook Academy of Art*

43. Triton Pool Court (South)

Eliel Saarinen, 1939; Peter Osler, landscape architect, restoration, 1998

The formal garden of the art academy is characterized by a series of gradual terraces, which are echoed by the descent of the garden pools. From the bottom of the stairs at the base of the propylaeum and the *Europa and the Bull* sculpture, the waters of the Triton Pool drop first to a middle-level pool and then to a lower-level pool that ends just north of the grassy area before the Nichols Gate.

Carl Milles's sculpture, *Europa and the Bull*, of 1915–1916, faces south from the terrace, while the four tritons, accompanied by the playful dolphins and other water creatures, frolic in the first of a series of pools. The Triton group, another of Carl Milles's works, dating from 1923–1924, creates a sense of moving perpetually and rhythmically down the axis of the garden. The carefully designed jets of water and the flow of the pool heighten the installation's dynamic quality. The original sculpture was erected in the market square of Halmstad, Sweden, in 1926. The Triton Pool was completely rebuilt to replicate the original structure in 1998. Peter Osler of Ann Arbor oversaw the restoration of the landscape.

44. Academy Quadrangle of the Museum and Library (North)   *Eliel Saarinen, 1939*

The huge scale of the paved walk, with its massive concrete slabs, relates sensitively to the quadrangle itself and to the building. It is an ample gathering place for visitors disembarking at the drop-off, and it contains a number of interesting sculptures.

Carl Milles's *Orpheus* fountain was sited and placed in its present form in 1938, two years before the creation of the propylaeum joining the museum and library. A regrouping of eight figures from one of Milles' major works—the *Orpheus* fountain for the Great Music Hall in Stockholm, Sweden—becomes, less its central heroic figure of Orpheus and the

Orpheus *Fountain, North Quadrangle, Cranbrook Art Museum and Library, Cranbrook Academy of Art*

pedestal image of Cerberus, a fresh and poetic composition in bronze and upward-shooting water. Milles selected the theme of music and presented a plan to render Orpheus, the Greek god of music. The larger-than-life figures are arranged in a circle looking outward, whereas in the Stockholm fountain they are tightly placed in a square configuration. Booth purchased the pieces of the *Orpheus* fountain he wanted, and, with Milles and Saarinen, sited the fountain along the axis created by the *Europa and the Bull* sculpture, the Triton Pool, and the Nichols Gate.

A sacred Chinese lion dog sculpture, dating from the fifth or sixth century, faces north and is seated on his haunches on a pedestal that divides the staircase east of the Academy Quadrangle. Originally the noble

Chinese Lion Dog sculptures, Cranbrook Academy of Art

and dignified animal may have been one of a pair of guardian lion statues. Lion sculptures once guarded entrances to palaces, homes, and sacred buildings in China. From its position on the northern ramp of the art academy museum, the lion dog marks the western axis from the West Terrace of Cranbrook House and Gardens and lends its name to the Ramp of the Chinese Lion Dog. In poses of maternal adoration and protection a sculpture of a pair of lynx with their young, by the sculptor Jussi Mantynen and done in the mid-1930s, flanks the broad stairs that lead from the circle drive to the art museum and library.

The installation of the *Orpheus* fountain and the construction of the Cranbrook Art Museum and Library represented at that time the culmination of the development of the art academy.

Kingswood Campus

45 | Main Entrance Gate and Oval Turning Circle
46 | Gate Lodge
47 | Kingswood School
48 | Wenger Gymnasium
49 | Headmistress's Residence (Robin Hill)

The Former Kingswood School for Girls

Kingswood is the masterpiece of the remarkable cultural and educational complex into which George Gough and Ellen Warren Scripps Booth transformed Cranbrook, their large farm estate in the rolling countryside of Bloomfield Hills.

The Kingswood Campus of Cranbrook Kingswood Upper School is located a short distance from the rest of the Cranbrook campus on a fifty-acre site in the northeastern section of what was originally the Cranbrook estate. It is approached from the Woodward entrance road and from Cranbrook Road, less than one mile north of Lone Pine Road. Nestled against a wooded hill, known as Angley Woods, the school lies in a grassy area that slopes gently down to the shores of Kingswood Lake; a stretch of the winding north branch of the River Rouge runs through the grounds. Athletic fields lie in the valley to the west, and a rim of hills separates the Kingswood campus from the Cranbrook campus further to the west.

In 1926 George Gough Booth thought that the first step taken in the development of the girls' school might be to build a new school building at the north end of the Brookside School campus. As the older girls graduated from Brookside School, possibly at the sixth grade, they would move to the day school. One to three years later, these girls would be ready for secondary schooling. By then a larger building might be ready on the property north of the lake, and Brookside School, having grown with the community, would take over the additional building for its regular work. After a day school for girls was started, it might be five years or more before the girls' school would be ready for boarding pupils in any considerable numbers.

The establishment of a girls' school at Cranbrook, supported by Ellen Warren Scripps Booth's gift of $200,000, was first initiated in 1928. George Booth, however, remained skeptical about the imminent need for a girls' school. Booth had written to the Cranbrook Foundation in September 1928, "I may say that we have only a very limited amount of evidence to prove to us that the Girls School is an immediate necessity. The demand may exist, but it is not evident, although none the less, I am still of the opinion that the time is not far distant when, if we are able to do so, the Foundation should undertake to provide for such an institution." The many discussions about establishing a girls' school finally moved forward when Mrs. Booth said their granddaughters needed a place to go to school that was equal to the boys' school.

During a stay in Santa Barbara, California, over the winter of 1928–1929, Booth's son Henry Booth made two preliminary sketch plans for the Kingswood School for girls, one for each of two prospective sites—the valley site to the north of Kingswood Lake that eventually was selected, and the site at the north end of Sunset Hill that later became the site of

Kingswood School (looking south)

Cranbrook Institute of Science. Only remnants of Henry Booth's plan survive in the Cranbrook Archives, but they suggest a school that was to have had a conservative, romantic appearance, more akin to Cranbrook School.

George Booth sketched out plans for a school on the north shore of Kingswood Lake and gave Eliel Saarinen the task of designing the school. Saarinen, who had just completed his house at the academy, worked closely with the Booths to determine the needs of the school for girls. Saarinen's design for Kingswood departs radically from his previous designs for Cranbrook School and for the art academy. His solution for Kingswood reflects the evolution of his own professional development over five years in the United States and the donors' wish that each Cranbrook institution have a unique visual character while harmonizing with the whole.

On the west end of the Kingswood School site stood a group of wood-frame shingle-roofed farm buildings erected by the Booths in 1904 and 1905 to the plans of Albert Kahn. A gambrel-roofed house, stables, sheep shed, water tower, dairy, chicken houses, a bull, calf and pigpen, sheds for a buggy and coaches, and a blacksmith shop were centered around a graveled court. Pasture and crop lands at Sunset Hill stretched west to the valley beyond. These buildings, abandoned in 1914 when farm operations were moved to the concrete block farm buildings on the site of Cranbrook School, were demolished in 1917–1918. The farmhouse remained until 1926, however, serving as rental housing.

In 1930 the Cranbrook Foundation proceeded with the organization of the secondary school for girls and the construction of buildings for its use. Booth regarded the Depression as a good time to build, because costs would be lower. The school was named Kingswood School-Cranbrook for Elizabeth Kingswood, George Gough Booth's paternal grandmother. In the 1930 agreement between the Cranbrook Foundation and its newly appointed trustees, the Booths outlined their desires for the school:

> that it shall provide for the moral and religious education of the youth committed to its care, as well as for their intellectual training; that it shall benefit by the best traditions of similar undertakings in the past and the clearest visions of the future; that it shall evidence a spirit of progress, and be open-minded in matters of education and religion; and that it shall enlist in its service persons qualified by experience to manage its temporal affairs, and also those competent to shape its educational policies.

The school would be so conducted to merit the approval of the Protestant Episcopal Church in the Diocese of Michigan. In addition to the other branches of its curriculum, which should be such as to offer a good general education, the school would provide opportunity for competent instruction in drawing, design, decoration, and the artistic handicrafts.

Costs for construction, equipment, and improvement of grounds were estimated at $2 million. Thus, buildings, land, and endowment of Kingswood School represented approximately $3 million or one-fifth of the $15 million the Booths invested in the development of the five educational institutions that made up the Cranbrook cultural center in Bloomfield Hills, and the church. The deeding of the Kingswood parcel completed the Booth's allocation of 225 acres of the Cranbrook estate. All the couple retained was a small portion reserved as their residential grounds.

Beginning in September 1930, classes for the newly founded school met in temporary quarters in the old Meeting House at Brookside School until the new building was completed and ready for occupancy in the fall of 1931. After a search of dozens of schools, Gladys Turnbach of Miss Hall's School in Pittsfield, Massachusetts, was named headmistress. She lasted only a few months, though, resigning, because, as she explained, she lacked the physical energy to cope with both operating the then extant school in the Meeting House and planning for all permanent arrangements in the new building. Thirty-five day students were enrolled at Kingswood that first year. Then the post sixth-grade academic program moved from its temporary quarters at Brookside to Kingswood's newly opened building. When it opened in September 1931, unlike other institutions at Cranbrook, Kingswood School was complete in its final form.

Katherine Rogers Adams, Ph.D., a graduate of Wellesley College and Cornell University and former professor of history and dean of the faculty of Mills College in California, succeeded Gladys Turnback and was principal and president of the school when it opened. She was succeeded in 1934 by Margaret Augur.

Margaret A. Augur served as headmistress for sixteen years from 1934 to 1950. Graduated from Rosemary Hall in Greenwich, Connecticut, Augur attended Bryn Mawr College and earned her B.A. degree at Barnard College. She pursued graduate work at the University of Chicago and at Columbia University and studied at the University of Grenoble, France. Before coming to Kingswood School, Augur was academic dean at Bradford Junior College.

"Enter to learn, go forth to serve" is the Kingswood motto. At the outset everyone was intent on the development of the school's spirit and traditions. The Kingswood School Cranbrook board of trustees was enraptured with the setting, building, and furnishings of the school they were privileged to oversee. In a letter of September 23, 1931, to the Booths they pledged their intent to make the school all the Booths wished it to be: "a vital educational institution, keenly sensitive and responsive to the needs of the individuals, the community and the state which you designed it to serve."

Today the Kingswood Campus of the Cranbrook Kingswood Upper School is the setting for humanities classes, fine arts and studio arts classes, and the dance studio; the girls' dormitories; and the middle school for girls. The administration and facilities staff is expending extraordinary effort in preservation planning and in executing these plans. In 1999–2000 the copper roof was replaced as a donation by the Christman Company.

45. Main Entrance Gate and Oval Turning Circle

Eliel Saarinen, 1930–1931

The historic main entrance to Kingswood is marked by three fluted capitals of Mankato limestone, grandly surmounting stone piers that anchor the wrought-iron gates. Walter Nichols crafted the wrought-iron gates after Eliel Saarinen's design. A similar pedestrian gate, also by Nichols, is to the south of the automobile entrance. While Cranbrook was designed for pedestrians, Kingswood was designed for arrival by automobile. The entrance road leads through the gates to an oval turning circle with a drop off before stairs rising to the main lobby entrance and to parking. The way to the dining room, auditorium, and residence foyer in the east wing is

Main Entrance Gates, Kingswood School

Entrance Oval, Kingswood School

marked by the procession of a fluted and tiered Mankato limestone colonnade, and by the intricate leaded glass window on the north. To the north, across the turning circle, a brick retaining wall holds the hillside back.

46. Gate Lodge *Cranbrook Architectural Office, 1931*

The gate lodge at Cranbrook Road secures the service entrances to the building. It is crafted with the same care as the main building. A panel of brick checkerwork set off by headers of brick tinted pale green encircles the building at the second story level. Originally designed by Fred Thompson of the Cranbrook Architectural Office in an English style to conform to other buildings along the road, Eliel Saarinen insisted the plans be revised in a prairie-style mode.

47. Kingswood School
Eliel Saarinen, 1930–1931; Edward A. Eichstaedt, landscape architect

The Kingswood School building consists of two connected groups of rectangular wings that form quadrangles, creating a succession of low projecting wings. A rectangular four-story central block or tower ringed with a frieze of leaded glass windows rises over the horizontal building as a symbol of scholastic authority. Plain fenestration, most of which consists of steel casement windows with hoppers and awnings, is augmented by decorative entrances and complex leaded glass windows. Stepped chimneys project above the otherwise low building. Telescoping fluted stone columns with capitals, paneled sections of brick, and leaded glass set off the formal spaces. The low pitched hipped roof with broadly overhanging eaves, the horizontal bands of windows, the spreading out of the building toward the periphery of the dramatic site on Kingswood Lake from the higher condensed center, and the open interior spaces are reminiscent of the Prairie style architecture of Frank Lloyd Wright. According to architecture critic Martin Filler, this fact led the historian Henry-Russell Hitchcock to regard Saarinen as Wright's chief rival in America.

The brick, stone, and copper harmonize beautifully in the exterior. Sand-molded bricks ranging from warm pale pink to light yellowish brown are laid in common bond, with every fifth course headers, raked horizontal joints, and flush vertical joints. Projecting stringcourses of brick headers tinted pale green encircle the building beneath the broad overhanging eaves and the windows. Soft yellowish orange Mankato limestone from the Breen Stone and Marble Company at Kasota, Minnesota, trims the exterior. Copper with standing seams, oxidized to a pale green, covers the roof.

The massing of the building is horizontal on a succession of levels to conform naturally to the slight slope of the land from the entrance court to the lake southward. The school dormitory is on the south side as that affords the best outlook but all the benefits of the east, south, and west exposures. A heavily wooded hill protects the entire building on the north side.

The school is arranged with three functional areas: the classroom or academic wing; the central area, including the auditorium and dining room; and the dormitory wing. The quadrangles form interior courts, and the wings reach out to embrace terraces. An easy and logical circulation system of corridors, foyers, lobbies, courts, and terraces, flows horizontally and vertically throughout the building.

The joined quadrangles and wings house study halls, studios, classrooms, administrative offices, residence and reception rooms, library, gymnasium, auditorium, and dining room. The residence rooms were designed for a single occupant, with one bath connecting two rooms. Everything desirable for a girls' school was contained within Kingswood School—studios and workrooms for music, drama, dancing, the arts and crafts, and domestic science, as well as classrooms and laboratories for academic subjects and college preparatory work.

At the Booths' suggestion the entire Saarinen family participated in creating Kingswood. This collaboration resulted in one of the most interesting projects in the history of contemporary American decorative arts. The school constitutes a unified whole with buildings, interiors, and furnishings designed and executed by diverse designers and craftsmen working in harmony under the guidance of master architect Eliel Saarinen. Saarinen's wife, Loja Saarinen, through her firm Studio Loja Saarinen, created curtains and upholstery fabrics, and supervised the weaving and execution of the tapestry her husband designed for the dining room. Loja Saarinen and Maja Andersson-Wirde also designed area rugs, woven by hand on the Cranbrook looms. Carpets needed in vast quantity were designed by Saarinen and Andersson-Wirde and put into machine production. Eero Saarinen, the Saarinens' son, designed special furniture, which were executed in models and produced in quantity. Eero also designed the leaded-glass windows. Eliel and Loja Saarinen's daughter, Pipsan Saarinen Swanson, created the interior decoration for the dining room, auditorium, ballroom, dormitory lounges, study hall ceilings, and other spaces.

The west wing or academic wing of Kingswood School is one story, but where the hill falls away to the south on the lake side, it exposes a lower level. One enters the west wing through the main covered entrance court to the Green Lobby. The lobby opens to administrative offices, classrooms, and hallways. The wide classroom corridor circumnavigates the interior of the wing overlooking the courtyard. The south portion of the west wing originally contained the library, which now serves as the common; the classroom corridor; and three study halls with a lobby between them, which today serves as the library. The north wing holds the busy arts and crafts and weaving studios. Terraces lie to the south and west, accessed by grand double doors of leaded glass.

The main courtyard is also known as the Diana Courtyard, because of the Carl Milles sculpture that serves as the central focus of the court. The *Diana* sculpture, from about 1928, is mounted on the main axis of the walkway to the covered entrance and the oval turning circle. The pose of the bronze dancer exudes lightness and grace.

A covered walkway leads to the main entrance of the Green Lobby, which was named for the lustrous green architectural tile, fired by Mary Chase Perry Stratton in the kilns of the Pewabic Pottery in Detroit, that once covered the room. It was replicated and relaid in 1999. The wainscot is paneled in the same dark green Pewabic tile highlighted by silver metallic tile stripes set in black mortar. A low tiled fireplace gives warmth to the lobby. The walls and ceilings are of sand-finish plaster painted flat gray and striped with green and white. The lobby sparkles with light diffused through the leaded glass of the windows and double doors. Lighting fixtures concealed in the cylindrical recesses of the ceiling are connected visually with a silver and turquoise green decoration painted by Pipsan Saarinen Swanson. An unusual brass banister rises on alternating stairs, opposes individual ceramic cups that substitute for a hand rail. (The original floor rug displayed a yellow and white pattern on a light green background).

Main entrance lobby (Green Lobby), West Wing, Kingswood School

The original three study halls and their connecting lobby now serve as the library. The library was remodeled to the plans of Tarapata, MacMahon, and Paulsen in 1980.

The east wing and central block of the school contain the service entrance, court, kitchen, dining room, a reception lobby and vestibule, auditorium, stage, and the lockers connecting the east wing to the west wing. The east wing also holds the infirmary.

Dining Room (looking east from Auditorium), Kingswood School

For special events the doors of the dining hall and the auditorium can be thrown open and the rooms linked by means of this lobby. This space also serves as the lobby to the dormitory area. The windows of the doors and the large north window are leaded and filled with light amber and green cathedral glass. The names of graduates are inscribed in the wall panels of the lobby and arranged by class year. A room above the lobby overlooks the dining room, auditorium, and vestibule.

The large vaulted dining room is the most famous space at Kingswood. Eight-paned steel casement windows on the north and south walls and a small row of leaded glass clerestory windows above admit light to the dining room. Pipsan Saarinen Swanson designed the interior oak finished in a dark acid-stain and sand-finish plaster walls and ceiling originally toned to a warm, flat gray—an airy neutral background for the contrasting furniture, tapestry, and lighting. Round tables and chairs designed by Eero Saarinen are of silver gray birch, but the chairs were originally striped with rosy vermilion and upholstered with a linen damask of the same color. The original textured and colored curtains of wool and rayon patterned in vermilion, silver, and gray no longer hang in the windows. The large *Festival of the May Queen* tapestry designed by Loja Saarinen and woven in green, coral, and creamy white coarse homespun linen and wool hangs on the east wall. A pair of columnar aluminum *torcheres* designed by Eliel Saarinen and topped by stylized peacocks flank the tapestry like ancient staffs of office. Metal floor lamps by Von Nessen stand along the north and south walls between the windows. The gracious dining of the 1930s to 1950s has given way to cafeteria-style food service.

Pipsan Saarinen Swanson decorated the interior of the auditorium. The acid-stained dark oak floor and oak wainscot; the oak pilasters stained light to wainscot height; the sand-finish plaster walls above the wainscot painted a light gray and decorated with silver leaf supply the warm neutral background for the interesting silver leaf decoration of the ceiling. The series of small dome coffers not only furnishes a reflecting surface for the suspended aluminum reflectors but also breaks the ceiling line for proper acoustics. The warm gray velour stage curtain ornamented in silver Fabikoid covers a back curtain of light green velour. Chromium plated chairs designed by Eero Saarinen are upholstered in light green.

Just as the auditorium, lobby, and dining room relate to each other horizontally, the auditorium relates to the practice rooms and dance hall above and the practice rooms below. Dramatics rooms are over the stage, a music corridor and classrooms are on the third floor over the reception lobby, and the dance hall is on the fourth floor.

Leaded glass windows surround the top portion of all four walls of the former ballroom. Pipsan Saarinen Swanson decorated the ceiling with star-embellished coffers, which gave the room its nickname, "Heaven." The narrow stairway leading to the ballroom restricted the flow of traffic, so the ballroom was rarely used for dances. During World War II George Booth ordered the space modified for residential use.

Off the corridor of the south wing of Kingswood are arranged reception rooms and pairs of dormitory rooms connected with baths. Eighteen dormitory rooms are on the first floor. The dormitory corridor is flanked by east and west terraces. The upper floors hold forty-nine student bedrooms or dormitory rooms with kitchenette, pressing room, and linen storage. This wing of the dormitory section also houses an infirmary.

Dark stained oak floor, wood trim painted with a light gray enamel, and sand plaster walls and ceiling painted light gray clad the interior of the dormitory reception room. The room was called the Rose Lobby, because everything was done in rose and coral colors.

The dormitory bedrooms were designed to harmonize with a basic scheme of yellow, rose, green, or blue. The floors are dark stained oak; the woodwork was painted a light gray enamel; the walls were sand-finish plaster, painted a light gray. This produced a cheerful simplicity that was both feminine and varied.

Saarinen created courtyards as open space delineated around the building with steps, fountains, sculptures, and pergolas. The infirmary court and terrace are circular. The interior dormitory courtyard is located between the dormitories and the dining hall. Piers with stacked, inverted, and telescoping fluted capitals support the roof over the stairs leading down to this courtyard. The south auditorium terrace, its stacked and fluted piers with stone capitals, overlooks the lake. It is accessed to the west from the reception lobby. Play fields (hockey fields and tennis courts) and other facilities are on the west.

Reception room, dormitory, Kingswood School

Two Sisters *sculpture by Marshall Fredericks, Alumnae Court at Wenger Gymnasium, Kingswood School*

48. Wenger Gymnasium   *O'Dell, Hewlett and Luckenbach, 1964–1965*

When Kingswood School opened, the gymnasium was located in the base-ment. But the space became cramped, and the noise from gym activities was transmitted upstairs easily. The Wenger Gymnasium, built in the 1960s and the gift of Henry E. and Consuela S. Wenger, is sited in the south ter-race of the academic wing that descended to a grassy plain. Designed in character with the existing buildings, the gym is constructed of the same

Two Girl's Dancing *sculpture by Carl Milles, Kingswood School*

warm pale pink to light grayish yellowish brown brick found in Kingswood School. With folding partitions its large space (112 × 75 feet) can be divided into two gymnasiums and a dance instruction room that can double as a stage. The building has an office.

Alumnae Court is tucked into the portion of the south terrace that remains. Having run out of space for listing the names of alumnae in the dining/auditorium reception lobby, inscription plaques bearing the names of graduates arranged for the classes of 1973 to the present line the exterior walls of this courtyard, giving the space its current name. The bronze *Two Sisters* sculpture created by Marshall M. Fredericks in 1965 is installed in a circular fountain in the courtyard opposite the main entrance to the gymnasium. The sculpture is a gift of Robert and Mary Alice Grindley.

A pathway between Wenger Gym and the main building leads down to the north shore Kingswood Lake and the bronze *Dancing Girls* sculpture by Carl Milles, executed in 1912–1913, opposite the boathouse.

In 1934 the Booths hired Edward A. Eichstaedt to landscape the Kingswood campus. At Kingswood Eichstaedt did the understory trees, water basins around Kingswood, and planting beds. A resident of Detroit whose work had slacked off during the Depression, Eichstaedt sought employment from the Booths at Cranbrook—hoping to work there, as he explained to Booth, "because of its artistic possibilities." College educated and trained by the prominent Jens Jensen in the theory and practice of broad scale naturalistic design, Eichstaedt had established his own practice in 1929. His work creating the broad sweeping naturalistic landscape for the great mansion of Alvin Macauley, president of Packard Motor Company—which was designed by Albert Kahn and built on Lake Shore Road in Grosse Pointe in 1929—and his twenty-five-acre park for the Kellogg Company in Battle Creek must have impressed Booth.

49. Headmistress' Residence (Robin Hill)

O'Dell, Hewlett and Luckenbach, 1951–1952

Robin Hill is located in Angley Woods atop of the hill. The brick and wood house was designed for the gracious living of the headmistress with rooms for entertaining, quiet living and study, and a maid.

Cranbrook Institute of Science

50 | Cranbrook Institute of Science and
     McMath Planetarium
51 | Cranbrook Institute of Science New Wing
     and Erb Family Science Garden

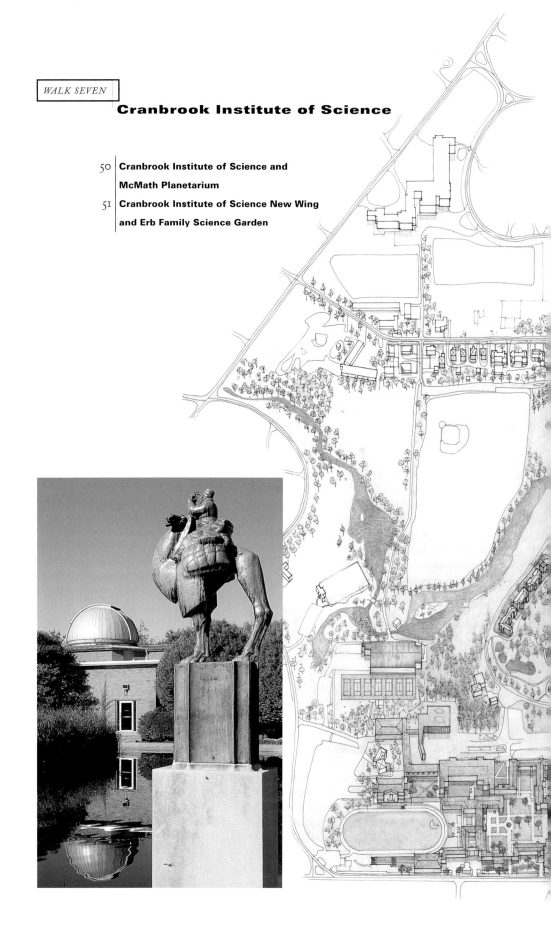

Natural History and Science Museum

Cranbrook Institute of Science is a nationally recognized natural history and science museum, primarily serving residents of Michigan and the Great Lakes region. It is housed in a building that was a masterpiece of Eliel Saarinen's modern designs, with a new wing by Steven Holl that forms one of the centennial construction projects outlined in the *Cranbrook Vision*. The science institute is reached by way of the Woodward entrance road.

At first science and nature studies at Cranbrook were supported by equipment, classrooms, and laboratories contained within the three schools. On occasion the boys selected the Cranbrook Academy Quadrangle fountain as the temporary home of turtles, goldfish, and black bass or carp.

Recognizing the need for a place for the boys to go in their free time to study plants, animals, and the natural environment, Cecil Billington, a trustee of the Cranbrook Foundation, and Lee A. White, a trustee of Cranbrook School, presented the problem to George Gough Booth. They argued for a simple, inexpensive, versatile, and preferably rustic structure, to be located somewhere down in the valley—where it would be obscured by the natural growth of shrubs and trees so as not to detract from the Saarinen buildings on campus. Here the boys could keep a rabbit, raccoon, snake, or turtle, and study its behavior. The structure might take the form of a laboratory, zoo, or even a taxidermist's workshop.

During the discussion Booth drew on a sketch pad a quadrangular structure that enclosed a court. To this he attached at one corner a circle, representing the dome of an observatory. He sent the sketch over to the Cranbrook Architectural Office for the preparation of detailed working drawings, and then Booth presented the matter of the science building to the Cranbrook Foundation board of trustees. In May 1930 the board authorized its construction, and in June it selected the Cranbrook Institute of Science as the name.

Booth chose Sunset Hill as the location of the institute, which was to be housed in a temporary cinderblock building, because its high siting and distance from other buildings enhanced astronomical viewing. Eliel Saarinen, who was not actively involved with the planning for the first science building, was opposed to locating any building in the center of the campus, preferring to keep the heart of Cranbrook parklike open space for people living on the grounds.

Sunset Hill and the land in the twenty-two acres of the Cranbrook homestead deeded to the Cranbrook Institute of Science lies in the north central part of the property, bounded by a residential development. The area consists of high morainal hills and slopes once scattered with elms and sumac, and includes the damp bottomland of a small branch of the River Rouge and the impoundment of a lower, longer section of the stream called

Kingswood Lake surrounded with red oak, elm, willow, and tamarack. The grounds would be used for nature study, including bird walks, bird nesting studies, and the banding of birds.

After the establishment of the Cranbrook Institute of Science in 1930, the Booths donated the Pohndorf Collection, a rare mineral collection that the couple had purchased in Denver, Colorado, in 1926. They shipped the collection back east to Cranbrook, but here it would require exhibition space. The Pohndorf Collection formed the nucleus around which the present mineral collection of the institute was built. The institute would also house the telescope initially installed in the Cranbrook School tower but removed because it did not function. Intended to enhance the scientific studies of Cranbrook students, the institute continuously increased in scope, accomplishments, renown, and more public roles.

The Cranbrook Institute of Science was managed by a board of directors that erected buildings for the institute and appropriated funds for the employment of staff and for equipment. In February 1932, because the institute amply demonstrated its usefulness as an integral unit in the Cranbrook Educational Community, the trustees of the foundation established the Cranbrook Institute of Science as a separate legal unit in the community, owning its lands, building, and personal property for endowment purposes.

The mission of the institute was to broaden human horizons by means of research and education in the natural and physical sciences. The 1932 articles of trust set forth these purposes:

> In addition to providing an observatory and a general science museum embracing exhibits illustrating as fully as may be the several branches of the Natural and Physical Sciences, primarily for the use and benefit of the institutions at any time in operation upon Cranbrook, the Institute shall encourage and develop the study of such Sciences and shall endeavor to advance the general knowledge thereof. It is the belief of the Donor [the foundation] that this branch of the Cranbrook educational group embraces great possibilities for future growth and genuinely beneficial influence not only to its immediate community but to science and to humanity as a whole, and it is the express hope of the Donor [the foundation] that through research, discovery and publication. The Cranbrook Institute of Science shall render an ever widening service for the betterment of mankind.

Science and art education formed an important part of the Cranbrook Schools—its directors desired that these subjects would have a lasting effect on the students enrolled here. *Precepts Governing Cranbrook,* written in 1934–1935, summarized the four-pronged purpose of the Cranbrook Institute of Science: "to develop Science in all the branches that are at present included in the Institute's program, and those that will be developed in the future; to arouse a general interest in Science; to provide the facilities for young scientists to do their research work under proper leadership; to help to organize and supervise the scientific activities of the schools."

A few years after the temporary building opened Eliel Saarinen prepared for Booth several different plans for a permanent building for the institute. In January 1933 Victor H. Cahalane, first director of the institute of science, suggested that the institute use the existing building for laboratories and offices and build an addition for exhibits. Booth thought this too modest a scheme. Saarinen felt that the most logical location for the institute would be along the periphery of the campus where public access would be direct. An area on the homestead property adjacent to Saint Dunstan's Playhouse and the Greek Theatre and near Cranbrook House seemed logical. Booth, too, examined the advantages of the site and felt that Cranbrook House and its surroundings might serve well as the new institute building. On closer look, he concluded that the cost of building a suitable observatory and modifying the chimneys of Cranbrook House and the neighboring buildings was impractical. Moreover, the realization that the visitors to the institute exceeded twenty thousand a year led him to reconsider his offer of the use of Cranbrook House. Ultimately, Saarinen was instructed in 1936 to design a new building on the site of the temporary cinderblock building of 1930.

The new building was to be a U-shaped structure north of the then existing building, connected by a partially walled arcade to the observatory— resheathed in brick, the only section of the old building to be retained. Both an exhibition building and a research center, the Saarinen building would hold the Hall of Minerals and the Hall of Man. The institute moved to temporary quarters in the basement of the pavilion, now Saint Dunstan's Playhouse, until the opening of the new institute on May 5, 1938.

From the outset, the location of the Cranbrook Institute of Science was troublesome. This remained so until the opening of the Woodward entrance to the campus in the mid-1990s. Situated at the very heart of the Cranbrook grounds, the institute had no direct access for its many visitors from the existing main roads. People traveling to the institute had to drive north up Academy Way and then meander through the grounds on the lesser Institute Way. In the 1930s Saarinen had suggested remedying this siting by locating the new permanent institute of science by Lone Pine Road so that ". . . all the institutions of a complete Cranbrook could have had their respective direct access from the street, and the park-grounds at the heart of the Cranbrook community would have been saved as a quiet place for all those living in the Community."

After the foundation was dissolved in 1973, the institute became a unit of the newly created Cranbrook Educational Community.

Skillman Wing and McMath Planetarium, Light Pylon and New Wing, Cranbrook Institute of Science

50. Cranbrook Institute of Science and McMath Planetarium

Cranbrook Institute of Science
> *George G. Booth, 1930; Eliel Saarinen, alteration and addition, 1936–1938*

McMath Planetarium   *William Edward Kapp, 1955*

Skillman Wing for Physical Sciences   *William Edward Kapp, 1960–1961*

Light Pylon (Light Tower)   *Eliel Saarinen and George Gough Booth, 1938*

Reflecting Pool with Mermaids and Tritons
> *Carl Milles, sculptor, designed 1925–1927, cast 1925–1934*

The first institute of science building was situated on high ground known as Sunset Hill at the head of a small ravine. Along the ravine were placed the cages of the "zoo." It was reached from Lone Pine Road by Academy and Institute Ways. The building was designed in 1930 by George Gough Booth as a temporary structure for developing the young institute of science program. Built in 1930–1931, it stood on the site of the present structure. The wood-shingled and concrete-block building was built around a square court. An open passage led into the central interior court, where a collection of boulders was exhibited. The astronomical observatory dome dominated the structure, and the observatory wing of the present building is the only surviving portion of the original; the rest was razed in 1936–1938 to make way for the present building. Saarinen's new building, which housed a series of educational dioramas, warehouse-like displays of minerals and fossils, and a domed astronomical planetarium, was opened on May 5, 1938.

Modern, simple, clean, and scientific in appearance, the U-shaped, horizontal building has a flat roof and bands of windows. An entrance porch, no longer in use, is on the south. The brick furnishes the primary ornamentation of the structure, which is one of texture. The

Skillman Wing and McMath Planaterium, Light Pylon and New Wing, Cranbrook Institute of Science

common brick, a mottled pale yellowish brown manufactured in Ohio, was by then known as "Cranbrook brick" for its frequent use here. The brick was laid over hollow tile in the exterior walls in a common bond with every sixth row being headers and the other rows being stretchers. The horizontal mortar joints of the brick were raked out to emphasize the strong horizontal lines of the building. For example, the concrete piers that support the south entrance porch, formerly the much wider open terrace that sheltered the main entrance and which is now enclosed to serve as the sunny south-facing Reflections Café, are incised with right angle and quarter rolls. These catch light and shadow and relieve the severity of the horizontal mass of the main structure. The simple, clean surface of the interior, like that of the exterior, projected the scientific nature and purpose of the institute.

Sixty feet in diameter, the McMath Planetarium was designed by William Edward Kapp, designer of Meadowbrook Hall, the Alfred G. and Mathilda Dodge Wilson Estate at Rochester Hill, and formerly of Smith, Hinchman, and Grylls, one of the nation's oldest architectural firms. The planetarium was dedicated to Robert R. McMath, president of Motors Metal Manufacturing Company, founder of the McMath-Hulbert Observatory, and an organizer of the science institute's board of directors in 1930, whose life interest was astronomy. By 1955 the multilevel science institute, excluding the planetarium wing, contained 539,000 cubic feet and had a floor area of 43,864 square feet with exhibit space, auditorium, meeting rooms, library, shops, and services space, offices, laboratories, and storage. In 1961–1962 the Skillman Wing, also designed by Kapp, was added to the institute. The wing was given in memory of Robert H. Skillman, vice president and director of Minnesota Mining and Manufacturing, by Rose P. Skillman and the Skillman Foundation.

The adjacent reflecting pool with the playful *Mermaids and Tritons* sculpture by Carl Milles animated the otherwise unadorned building in a powerful but serene way. A *Pair of Running Boars* sculptures by Carl Milles greeted visitors arriving at the former main entrance, and *Sven Hedin on a Camel,* also by Milles, seemed to look out for their arrival up Institute Way. The very popular *Stegosaurus* sculpture—not a work of art but a sculpture needed in front of

Mermaids and Tritons *sculpture by Carl Milles, Skillman Wing and McMath Planetarium*

every science museum—thrills young visitors and anticipates the Tyrannosaurus Rex dinosaur and mastodon that await in the main gallery.

51. Cranbrook Institute of Science New Wing and Erb Family Science Garden

Cranbrook Institute of Science New Wing *Steven Holl, 1997–1998*
Erb Family Science Garden *Peter Osler, landscape architect, 1997–1998*

By the end of the twentieth century, the Cranbrook Institute of Science faced increasing pressures on its facilities and programs. It had difficulty accommodating its growing numbers of visitors, and the programs it could hold did not meet their changing needs and expectations. Cranbrook required a new museum with exhibits that emphasized active learning. A few problems with the Saarinen building also needed correction: circulation between wings, which was hindered by the U-shaped plan; and a lack of natural light inside resulting from a conservative approach to exhibitions. Called for was an addition to and rehabilitation of the existing institute, one that would reflect the institute's mission to provide excellent science education and to improve its strategic position as an important regional natural history and science museum.

In 1976 James Alfred and Florence Louise Booth Beresford presented a gift toward the renovaton and expansion of the institute of science;

Institute of Science

over time they increased this gift. Twenty years later Fred and Barbara Erb presented a $1 million challenge grant to the institute. These donations inspired further contributions to fund the new addition, one of five construction projects articulated in the *Cranbrook Vision*.

The Cranbrook architectural advisory council recommended Steven Holl of New York City to design the addition to the Cranbrook Institute of Science. An architect known for sensitive additions to existing structures, Holl shared Saarinen's interest in the theoretical issues of science, the use of craft, and the integration of architecture, art, and nature. As then president Lillian Bauder explained: "Steven sustains the search for form that Eliel Saarinen set in motion at Cranbrook. I was struck particularly by his ability to create a scheme for a building that, when placed on the campus design, looked as if it had been there always. Steven captured the genius of Saarinen and fused it with his own striking vision."

Steven Holl (1947–) teaches in the graduate school of architecture at Columbia University and has taught at Syracuse University, the Parsons School of Design, and the University of Washington. He graduated with honors from the University of Washington, studied architecture in Rome in 1970, and took post-graduate work at the Architectural Association in London in 1976. Holl established Steven Holl Architects in 1976 in New York. He is an international designer with projects in the United States, Finland, the Netherlands, Germany, Switzerland, and Japan. Holl is known for taking a geometrical approach to his work and for paying attention to detail, especially in the selection of materials. He considers postmodernist architecture overly decorative and thinks modernists fail to recognize the sensual elements of construction. Michael Graves, in a 1987 *Architectural Record* article, grouped Holl with Eero Saarinen, Charles Eames, and Frank O. Gehry, and stated that Holl "reveals the expressive potential of technology." Steven Holl Architects won the design competition for the Helsinki Museum of Contemporary Art in Finland, which was completed in 1998. The firm was selected to design an addition to the University of Virginia's architecture school. In 1995 the New York Chapter of the American Institute of Architects awarded Holl a Design Award for his design of the Cranbrook Institute of Science.

At the outset of the project in 1990 Steven Holl began thinking about the possibilities presented by a science museum built for the twenty-first century, examining the original building and deciding how to best preserve the Saarinen architectural legacy. For three years the firm worked on designs and then drafted drawings. He stated, "Our aim is to make the least intrusion on the architecture of the original Saarinen building while maximizing the potential for future circulation and visiting experiences with the addition."

On September 7, 1996, O'Neal Construction broke ground for the new Cranbrook Institute of Science wing. By April 1997 the erection of the steel, masonry, and glass forming the structure was underway. By late Fall, the walls were up, and the heating, ventilating, plumbing, and electrical systems were installed. In 1998 the plaster, paint, and trim finished the structure, and that summer the addition opened. New exhibits were installed and renovations to the original Saarinen wing were finished by the end of 1999.

The new addition is a dynamic adjunct and companion piece to the original science museum expanded by Saarinen in 1936–1938. Its own U-shaped plan nestles within and straddles like a toggle joint the wings of Saarinen's building so as to lightly connect with and form an interior courtyard with the older building, into which the Erb Family Science Garden is placed. The observatory from the old wing, the planetarium, and the entrance tower of the new wing project outward from the low, horizontal mass. The glass-block pylon rises from a point between the institute and the parking lot. Adding twenty-seven thousand square feet of space to the institute, this is among the largest of the five *Cranbrook Vision* projects.

Light Mankato limestone quarried at Kasota, Minnesota, and pale brown concrete blocks rise in the exterior walls of the new wing to a flat roof. An acid-reddened brass canopy shelters the doors to the Light Laboratory entry tower. The northwest corner of the addition is cantilevered to allow the gently sloping interior garden to spill out under the building toward the wooded valley below and the nature trails beyond so that the building mingles with nature and nature permeates the building.

Light Pylon, Cranbrook Institute of Science

High ceilings create grand interior spaces. Inside are spacious exhibit halls with state-of-the-art technology. The old and new sections blend into one institute, which features four new exhibit halls, five renovated exhibit halls, improved teaching spaces, a multimedia science information center, new exhibits, and a science garden with overhead water-ways. The first floor has the Connections Theater, and the mastodon and Tyrannosaurus Rex dinosaur exhibits. A rooftop terrace affords visitors views of the surrounding Cranbrook campus. The ground floor contains changing exhibition space, an auditorium, a sit-around, water passage, and classrooms. The original wing contains five renovated exhibition halls and a storage area for the institute's extensive collections.

Through the canopied entrance, visitors enter the Institute of Science by way of the spectacular sparkling and prismatic Light Laboratory. The exterior of this three-story tower is clad in Mankato limestone with a staggered grid of mullions that frame seven different kinds and sizes of handcrafted glass—including convex, dappled, crinkled-like, and accordion. Light through the glass casts variously refracted, diffused, and prismatic rainbows of color—constantly changing and shadowing patterns on the white interior walls. The tower is both a Light Laboratory and a luminous foyer that leads to the Beresford Lobby and presents a view of the Erb Family Science Garden. The lobby gives access to the exhibition gallery, and by ramps and stairs to the historic building.

The long-term or permanent exhibitions gallery is skylighted. Its walls are covered with large sheets of perforated plywood. The floor is constructed of "concrete planks," each one spanning the thirty-eight-foot width of the hall. A wall of interlocking translucent glass panels admits daylight the full length of stairs that descend from the first-floor lobby and from the long-term or permanent exhibitions gallery to the ground-floor changing exhibitions gallery. From the exterior at night this wall glows with bands of soft red and greenish yellow.

Reception Lobby and Permanent Exhibition Space, New Wing, Cranbrook Institute of Science

The structure of the building and its elements are consciously revealed to the observer. In unexpected places one steals peeks of the mason's trowel mark left on the concrete floor of the exhibit areas, unfinished marks on molded sheet metal benches, and the wood forms, cracks, patches, and aggregate of the poured concrete foundation.

Holl paid special attention to selecting details and crafting items like the handcrafted brass door claps, folded brass light fixtures, hand railings, and lightly brushed and molded aluminum benches. The walls are joyously plastered with rough Pompeian red stucco, and they oppose the expanses of translucent interlocking glass planks that line stairs descending to the lower gallery.

Under the direction of Dan Hoffman, the Cranbrook Architectural Office created many of the details and structures in the new building. One of these is the wooden igloo-shaped Connections Theater in the "Our Dynamic Earth" exhibit, which serves as a video projection booth that orients visitors to the organizing theme of the museum.

The new building improves access and circulation by opening the dead-end corridors and galleries of the earlier building, and admits abundant daylight to the interior. It doubles the area of Saarinen's science center courtyard and integrates itself with the surrounding landscape.

The Erb Family Science Garden, designed by landscape architect Peter Osler, is situated in the newly created courtyard—enclosed by the U-shape of the new Holl wings, and which are attached in a staggered manner to the U-shape of the old Saarinen building. Amidst a lively garden of native Michigan plants that reveal seasonal changes, the science garden displays water for which the Great Lakes state is famous—water in its liquid, vapor, and solid state. Beginning with its source in a long, narrow fountain, water flows over a transparent bottom through which wave patterns project onto a room below and which serves as a skylight to the water passage exhibit below. The flow pool drops in stages of three terraces. As it enters a compact, roofless concrete outdoor chamber called the "House of Vapor," mist wafts from the floor. Just beyond the end of the water passage is the "House of Ice." Fifteen feet in width and thirty feet in height, the teardrop-shaped, cage-like structure is open for visitors to enter. Ice forms over the mist sprayed on its surface resembling the ice caves in a glacier or the ice floes near the shores of the Great Lakes in winter. The science garden is

Erb Family Science Garden, Cranbrook Institute of Science

"House of Ice," Erb Family Science Garden

planted with diverse Michigan trees, shrubs, grasses, and flowers: fir, tamarack, shadblow (Juneberry), shumac, phitzer junipers, blueberry bushes,
osier dogwood, wild rose, maidenhair fern, whorlyflower, coneflowers, and
Solomon's heel. Indigenous ivy climbs on a wall constructed of stones contained in a wire mesh that runs the full length of the lowest pool. Many of
the plant materials were furnished by the Woodland Wildflower Rescue
Program of the Cranbrook House and Gardens Auxiliary. This courtyard
landscape connects with the larger landscape beyond. The gently sloping
interior garden spills out under the cantilevered northwest corner of the
addition toward the wooded valley, weaving together the picturesque landscape and the open courtyard.

The Holl building relates to the Saarinen building in wondrous
ways: the color of the materials, the creation of one masterful large central
courtyard with a Michigan theme, the integration of the architecture with
its natural surroundings as displayed in the wandering of the science garden into the valley, the echoing of the Light Laboratory and the Light Pylon
and the relating of the entrance point to the outdoor parking circle, the
preference for longer narrow buildings over wide bulky masses, and the
meticulous attention to exquisite detail.

Bloomfield Hills, Birmingham, Warren, and Fenton

52 | Lone Pine Inn (Parke-Lone Pine House)

53 | Robert and Eva-Lisa Saarinen Swanson House (Towerknoll)

54 | Vaughn-Saarinen House

55 | Eero Saarinen and Associates Office

56 | Greenwood Cemetery

57 | Birmingham City Hall and Library

58 | General Motors Technological Center

59 | Fenton Community Center

Note: Walk Eight is actually a driving tour

Loja Saarinen's House and Studio, Eero Saarinen, 1950, Bloomfield Hills

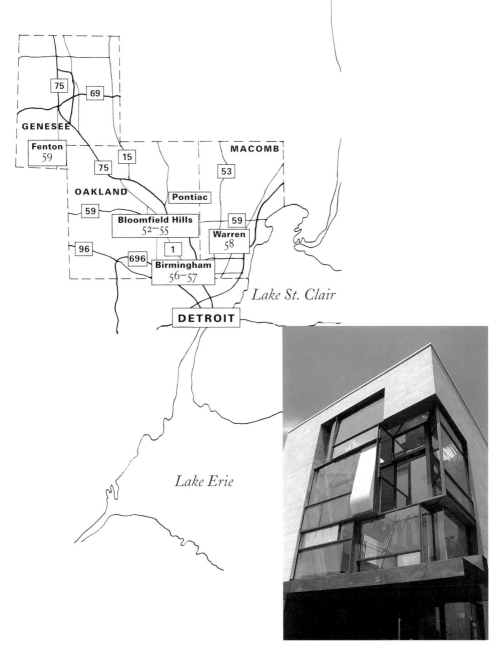

Lake St. Clair

Lake Erie

Bloomfield Hills, Oakland County

Bloomfield Hills is a residential community dotted with the estates and large houses of many wealthy Detroiters. In 1819 Amasa Bagley followed an Indian trail into this area and cleared land for a farm on the site of the city's present business section at the intersection of Woodward Avenue and Long Lake Road. Others followed, establishing the village of Bagley's Corners. In 1830, the village was renamed Bloomfield Center. In the early 1890s, city people began to move in and purchase farms in the area. The Booths arrived in 1904. The name of the village was changed to Bloomfield Hills. In 1927 it was incorporated as a village, and in 1932 a city.

52. Lone Pine Inn (Parke-Lone Pine House) *1830*

Ezra Parke, father of Hervey C. Parke who was co-founder of the Parke-Davis Pharmaceutical Company, built this house—located at the northwest corner of Woodward Avenue and Lone Pine Road. A home for his family, it also served as the local post office. George Gough Booth acquired the house in 1910 and enlarged it to nearly its present size with the addition of a large wing overlooking Lone Pine Road. From 1912 to World War I, the house functioned as the Bloomfield Hills Seminary, a day school for boys and girls organized by the Booths and their neighbors. From 1920 until the Depression, the house functioned as the Lone Pine Inn and Tea House, which served country-style cooking. Winifred Eastman, who had leased the property from Booth, operated the inn from the house and a small lodge-like structure that had been built in 1910 to function as a station for the electric interurban.

Lone Pine Inn, Bloomfield Hills

Booth gave the land and buildings to the Cranbrook Foundation during the Depression. The foundation divided the house into apartments for faculty. In 1973, the buildings were sold and slated for demolition to accommodate a large office complex. J. Robert F. Swanson and his son, Ronald, intervened to save the historic buildings, and in 1976, the city of Bloomfield Hills designated the complex as a historic district. RE/MAX restored the house for use as a real estate office.

53. Robert and Eva-Lisa (Pipsan) Saarinen Swanson House (Towerknoll)

J. Robert F. Swanson, circa 1926

This towered brick house, located at 955 Lone Pine Road (southeast intersection of the corner of Lahser Road), is Swanson's personal expression of the neo-Tudor style. While the Saarinen House was under construction, Swanson's wife's parents, Fliel and Loja Saarinen, lived in an apartment within Towerknoll.

Towerknoll (Robert and Eva-Lisa Saarinen Swanson House), Bloomfield Hills

Vaughan-Saarinen House, 1860-1870, Bloomfield Hills

54. Vaughn-Saarinen House (Peter Vaughan House)
1860–1870

The interior of this nineteenth-century Italianate farmhouse, originally the house of early Bloomfield Hills Township resident Peter Vaughan, was reduced to simple modern terms and furnished with a few pieces of modern furniture for the requirements of Eero Saarinen and his family. His marriage to ceramist Lily Swann ended in divorce in 1953, the same year he married art critic Aline B. Louchheim. His children included Eric and Susan by his first wife, and Eames by the second marriage. The house, located at 1045 Vaughan Road, was the scene of annual Christmas parties, luncheons, dinners, and cocktail and dinner parties for such visitors as Harry Weese, Charles Eames, Buckminster Fuller, Louis Kahn, and Marcel Breuer, to which his entire office staff was invited. After the death of his father in 1950, Eero designed a small glass and plywood house and studio at the rear of the property for his mother, Loja Saarinen.

Born in Finland, Eero Saarinen came to the United States with his parents in 1923. He studied architecture at Yale University from 1930 to 1934 and traveled throughout Europe for two years following graduation. He received the Michigan Society of Architects Gold Medal in 1959 and the American Institute of Architects Gold Medal posthumously in 1962.

55. Eero Saarinen and Associates Office

Eero Saarinen and Associates, 1950s

This building, located at 91 West Long Lake Road, served as architectural offices for Eero Saarinen and Associates after 1950. His second wife, art critic Aline Saarinen, described the one-story building as a "stark, workman-like glass and brick office." Saarinen had previously worked in partnership with his father across the street, and, in fact, they had collaborated on projects much earlier. In 1940 George Gough Booth suggested the termination of the Saarinens' relationship with the art academy and the removal of their architectural practice from the academy estate. Eero Saarinen and Associates was formed in 1950. Many outstanding architects would work for the firm: Robert Venturi, John Dinkeloo, Kevin Roche, Gunnar Birkerts, Cesar Pelli, Glen Paulsen, Leonard S. Parker, and Charles Bassett. In this building Eero Saarinen began all his landmark projects—the Trans World Airlines Terminal at Kennedy Airport, formerly New York International Airport; the Dulles International Airport in Washington, D. C.; Bell Telephone Laboratories, at Holmdel, New Jersey; Administration Headquarters for Deere and Company in Moline, Illinois; and the Jefferson National Expansion Memorial (Gateway to the West arch) in Saint Louis, Missouri.

After Saarinen's untimely death in 1961, the firm executed the architect's plans to move the office from Bloomfield Hills to Hamden, Connecticut. The move east—to a huge remodeled 1906 crenellated brick house—was precipitated by the desire to be nearer to the many consultants with whom the architects collaborated. Kevin Roche, John Dinkeloo, and Associates was the successor to Eero Saarinen's practice.

Eero Saarinen and Associates Offices, Eero Saarinen and Associates, 1950s, Bloomfield Hills

Birmingham, Oakland County

Situated along the Saginaw Trail (now Woodward Avenue and Michigan 1), Birmingham was a predominantly agricultural community during the nineteenth century. The advent of the railroad in 1839 and the electric interurban in 1896 linked Birmingham with Detroit. Roswell T. Merrill, the foundry owner, first applied the name Birmingham to the town in 1832 in the hope it would—like its English namesake—thrive as a place of industry. Platted in 1836, its post office was named Birmingham in 1838, it was incorporated as a village in 1864, and as a city in 1933.

The shift to a suburban community began in the early twentieth century after the Booths acquired Cranbrook. Birmingham grew rapidly in the 1920s. Then Woodward Avenue was widened, and Hunter Boulevard, now called Woodward, was developed into an eight-lane bypass around downtown. Residential development increased after World War II, along with religious, civic, and commercial construction. Birmingham's population in the year 2000 is over 20,000 residents, which has caused an upsurge in the construction of apartments and offices.

56. Greenwood Cemetery,

Oak Street two blocks west of North Old Woodward Avenue, Booth Burial Plot, Section D, Lot 20

The gravestones of George Gough Booth and Ellen Warren Scripps Booth feature the Booth and Scripps families shields—the three-bee shield, and the two bee and horseshoe shield, respectively. Their graves are surrounded by those of four of their children and their children's spouses: Warren Scripps Booth and Alice Newcomb, Henry Scripps Booth and Carolyn Farr Booth, James Alfred Beresford and Florence Louise Booth, and James Scripps Booth. Inscriptions and art work, designed by Harry Scripps Booth, personalize each of their gravestones.

Gravestones, Booth Burial Plot,
Greenwood Cemetery, Birmingham

Birmingham City Hall, Marcus R. Burrowes, 1928

57. Birmingham City Hall and Library

Marcus R. Burrowes, 1928

The neo-Tudor city hall and library opened as part of an ambitious civic center plan. They were designed by the architect who planned so many of Booth's farm buildings at Cranbrook.

58. General Motors Technological Center

Eero Saarinen and Associates, 1950–1957

General Motors Technological Center

The GM Technical Center, bounded by Mound Road, Thirteen Mile Road, Van Dyke (Michigan 53), and Twelve Mile Road, is a research center for the technical staff of the General Motors Company. General Motors desired an idyllic campus setting that would foster creativity. The company conceived of the idea in the 1930s, fenced in the newly acquired 900-acre site in 1942, and commissioned Eliel and Eero Saarinen to plan its design and development in the mid-1940s. World War II, however, and the postwar strikes and concentration of efforts on the conversion to peacetime automobile production, delayed construction. Eliel died in 1950, and the project passed to Eero, who designed the center. It opened in 1957.

Research laboratories and engineering, environmental, manufacturing, and design buildings are arranged around a huge rectangular lake. The long, low, Miesian structures are built of metal and glass with mass-produced, glazed, modular curtain-wall units. The visual strength of these buildings comes from the ceramic brick glazed to the formulae of Maija Grotell of the Cranbrook Academy of Art in brilliant reds, ultramarine, and burnt oranges and laid with grout of matching colors on the end walls of most buildings. The gleaming stainless steel water tower rises 138 feet from the north end of the lake, casting a reflection of itself. Through this image shoot sprays of water. The round aluminum dome of the Styling Building Auditorium is at the lake's southwest corner. The whole is placed on a ground of grass through which a roadway circumnavigates the campus and is surrounded by thousands of trees.

The site plan, the positioning of the elements at the center, the distances between them, and the vistas were suggested by Eliel Saarinen. Eero Saarinen, who took over the project after his father's death in 1950, designed the complex. The campus expresses a high-precision, mass-production, metal industry. Today, General Motors is undertaking a massive rehabilitation of the complex, utilizing the provisions of the federal historic preservation income tax credits.

59. Fenton Community Center *Eliel Saarinen, 1937–1938*

This crisp and clean light brown brick community center stands on the banks of the Shiawassee River in the heart of this small agricultural and manufacturing village. In December 1936 the Horace H. Rackham and Mary A. Rackham Fund appropriated to the village $200,000 for the construction of a modern structure for recreational, civic, and educational enterprises and $145,000 for maintenance and operation. Horace Rackham was one of the twelve original stockholders in the Ford Motor Company, and Fenton was the childhood home of his widow, Mary. Eliel Saarinen, with his son Eero Saarinen as consultant, designed the community center. The building is arranged with two levels; the rear is open to a view of the river. The low, horizontal massing and flat roofs with extended eaves are intersected by the vertical motif of the large chimney and of the regularly spaced windows. Open brickwork gives textural interest to the front. The building contains an auditorium, banquet hall, recreation hall, and meeting rooms.

Fenton Community Building

Detroit Landmarks

60 | Trinity Episcopal Church

61 | Detroit News Building

62 | Detroit Club

63 | Albert and Ernestine Kahn House

(Detroit Urban League)

64 | Saint Paul's Cathedral

65 | Detroit Institute of Arts

66 | Center for Creative Studies

67 | Scarab Club

68 | Pewabic Pottery

Note: Walk Nine is actually a driving tour

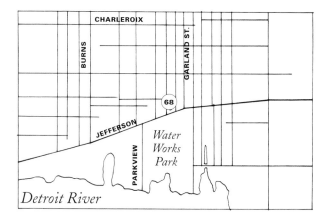

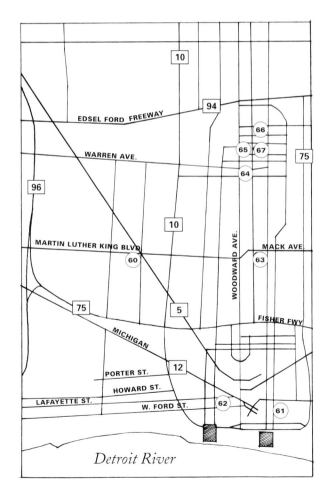

Detroit River

Detroit Arts and Crafts

The burgeoning industrial city of Detroit attracted artists, architects, and businessmen, many of whom were from England and came to Detroit by way of Canada. Caught up in the Arts and Crafts movement, they believed that the m tonous standardization of industrial methods was detrimental to society, and they sought to remedy the situation through good design. George Gough Booth, who came with his father from Saint Thomas, Ontario, to Detroit in 1881, would lead the Arts and Crafts movement in Detroit.

Both Booth's father and grandfather had been coppersmiths in Kent, England. In Windsor, Ontario, Booth owned an ornamental iron foundry. After marrying Ellen Warren Scripps, the daughter of newspaper magnate James Edmund Scripps and Harriett Josephine Messenger Scripps in 1887, Booth was convinced by his father-in-law to sell the iron works and manage the *Detroit News.* After the death of James Scripps in 1906, Booth became president of the newspaper.

60. Trinity Episcopal Church *Mason and Rice, 1890–1892*

James Edmund Scripps and his wife Harriet Josephine Messenger Scripps were the benefactors of this Late Gothic Revival church, located at 1519 Martin Luther King Boulevard. Publisher of the *Detroit Evening News*, later the *Detroit News*, Scripps was regarded as a connoisseur of art and architecture. The Scripps's purpose in rejecting Victorian romanticism in favor of a return to historical accuracy was to stimulate in church architecture a return to the older and more artistic forms. The Scrippses engaged an English architect to supply Mason and Rice with archaeological evidence and drawings of details from late fourteenth- and early fifteenth-century southern English churches. Mason and Rice incorporated them in this design, which follows the ecclesiological doctrine. The church stood within view of the Scripps and Booth houses.

Executed in rock-faced limestone trimmed with buff sandstone, the church has a cruciform plan with a massive square tower at the crossing. Prominent battlements, buttresses, tracery, gargoyles, and other carved-stone ornaments enhance the church's medieval character.

Entrance to the church is through a side porch. The pulpit and reading desk are properly located, and the choir is in the chancel. The interior combines the massive pillars of Norman churches with Gothic arcades throughout. Ten stone angels carved in Bedford limestone spring from side walls to support the nave beams beneath the wooden ceiling. The stained-glass chancel window showing the baptism of Christ is by Mayer and Company of Munich. The stained-glass window in the west aisle repre-

Trinity Episcopal Church, Mason and Rice, 1890–1892

senting Christ as the Good Shepherd and the memorial window to William Scott in the east aisle were manufactured by the Tiffany Glass Company of New York.

The present church replaced a board-and-batten Gothic Revival church of 1880 named Epiphany Reformed Episcopal Church—which was the site of the marriage of George Gough Booth and Ellen Warren Scripps in 1887. The congregation of Trinity (and Epiphany Reformed) was organized as Emmanuel Reformed Episcopal Church in 1879 and was renamed several times.

61. Detroit News Building   *Albert Kahn, 1915–1917*

As supervisor of the design, construction and equipping of the Detroit News Building, George Gough Booth was determined that it "possess dignity of style, chastity of spirit and substantiality appropriate to an institution which is aware of its intimate association with the welfare of the individual and the state."

The solid and massive stone building expresses its concrete frame through its piers and spandrels. The stone exterior is unadorned except for inscriptions carved in the parapet that speak of the declared functions and high purposes of the press; heraldic shields on spandrels below the third floor windows that are carved with the colophons or printers' marks of master craftsmen, including Albrecht Dürer, Richard Grafon, and Hugh Singleton; and carved heads of pioneers in printing—Johannes

Need caption here, Detroit News Building, etc.

Gutenberg, Christophe Plantin, William Caxton, and Benjamin Franklin, on the tops of the four piers.

When completed in 1917, the building was the largest exclusive newspaper plant in the world. It contains a power plant, business offices, editorial offices, conference rooms, reference room and library, art department, composing room, press room, mailing and shipping rooms.

In 1918, within one year of occupying the building, the *Detroit News* began construction of a seven-story paper storage warehouse on Fort Street and Third Avenue. This concrete and steel building is clad with gray vitrified face brick and trimmed with limestone. In 1929 an addition to the News Building doubled its size.

62. Detroit Club   *Wilson Eyre, Jr., 1891*

Founded in 1882 to provide a meeting place and luncheon service for the city's business and professional men, including George Gough Booth and many of Detroit's political and commercial leaders, this club was originally located in a converted private residence. When this proved inadequate, members purchased this site at 712 Cass Avenue and hired Wilson Eyre, Jr., a prominent Philadelphia establishment architect known particularly for his residential work, to design this new building.

Detroit Club, Wilson Eyre, Jr., 1891

The Detroit Club is a simplified version of Eyre's C. B. Moore House (1890) in Philadelphia. The symmetrical four-level Richardsonian Romanesque edifice has the medieval turret-like end bays that were a prominent feature of the wooden Queen Anne in America. The walls of the first story are constructed of rough, rock-faced Marquette brownstone and the upper stories of elongated red Roman brick. The interior contains a sitting room, a library, and a grill on the first floor; card rooms on the second; public and private dining rooms on the third; and sleeping rooms on the fourth. The building features high ceilings, finely crafted woodwork, and elegant furnishings. The semi-oval main dining room occupies both third- and fourth-floor space on the southeast end of the building. Richly paneled in dark wood, it has a small interior balcony and a huge fireplace flanked by wooden Corinthian columns.

63. Albert and Ernestine Krolik Kahn House
(Detroit Urban League)

Albert Kahn, 1906; gallery and garage addition, 1928

Albert Kahn, the architect of Cranbrook House, designed this house for himself and his wife and four children. The two-story house is constructed with Truscon reinforced-concrete floors. Named for the Trussed Concrete Steel Company (formed by Kahn's brother, Julius Kahn), the reinforced concrete and tile formed a flat ceiling over each floor and wood sleepers provided above permitted the nailing of finished wood floors. Red brick laid in English bond and trimmed with stone rises in the exterior walls through the first story; the second story is finished in stucco. Slate covers the hipped roof. A wooden door bordered with rosettes beautifully carved by Austrian-American wood-carver and modeler Joseph Jungwirth is recessed beneath an arched hood in the center of the front.

The interior is spacious and open in plan, and the very large windows, which later feature in Kahn's industrial designs, admit ample light and air. The stair hall and the reception, dining, and living rooms are lined with wood paneling. Jungwirth carved the mantelpiece and some portions of the furniture that Kahn designed for the house. In 1928 a large gallery was added at the southwest to accommodate the Kahns' social and business activities and their library and art collection. This room is paneled with wood and decorated with an ornamental plaster ceiling. After Kahn's death the Detroit Urban League acquired the house, located at 208 Mack Avenue.

Albert Kahn House, Albert Kahn, 1906

Saint Paul's Cathedral, Ralph Adams Cram, 1908–1911

64. Saint Paul's Cathedral
(Cathedral Church of Saint Paul/
Saint Paul's Protestant Episcopal Cathedral)

Ralph Adams Cram, 1908–1911

In 1906, two years after Saint Paul's Church officially became the Bishop's Church, it was offered the opportunity to establish a cathedral. Ralph Adams Cram of Cram, Goodhue and Ferguson of Boston and New York was called on to design a building suitable and appropriate as a cathedral for the diocese. Samuel Simpson Marquis, who served as rector of Saint Paul's Church during planning and construction of the cathedral, later put this experience to work at Christ Church Cranbrook.

The limestone Gothic Revival cathedral has a narrow-gabled and buttressed nave with side aisles, clerestory, and transepts. A rose window is positioned over the pointed-arch entry portal between projecting buttresses that support pinnacles. A large square tower designed to rise over the crossing was never built.

In the nave of the grand interior a pointed-arch arcade rests on smooth columns.

Four huge cylindrical piers at the crossing of the nave and transepts were intended to carry the tower. Artists and craftsmen who later would enhance Christ Church furnished decorative ornamentation for Saint Paul's Cathedral: William F. Ross and Company of Cambridge, Massachusetts, did the woodwork; John Kirchmayer of Oberammergau carved the reredos, the bishop's seat, the dean's stall, and lectern; and Mary Chase Perry Stratton manufactured at her Pewabic Pottery the tile floor with brown, pale brown, and blue glazes. In Saint Paul's Cathedral Ralph Adams Cram expressed through modern forms the spirit of the Gothic.

Detroit Institute of Art, Paul Philippe Cret and Zantzinger, Borie and Medary, 1927

65. Detroit Institute of Arts

Paul Philippe Cret and Zantzinger, Borie and Medary, 1927; Eleanor and Edsel Ford [South] Wing, 1963–1966; Jerome P. Cavanaugh [North] Wing, Gunner Birkerts and Associates, and Harley, Ellington, Cowin, and Stirton, 1970–1971; Main Entrance, Kiley-Walker Designs of Vermont, 1981

James Edmund Scripps, publisher of the *Detroit News,* supported the Detroit Museum of Art with a gift of its first old masters, and the Booth family continued this patronage. It was Scripps's hope that Detroit would become the art center of the West. The Richardsonian Romanesque Detroit Museum of Art (1888) by James Balfour of Hamilton, Ontario, which preceded this building, and its collection would make this happen.

With Ralph Harman Booth, George Gough Booth's brother, as its first president, the Detroit Arts Commission was formed in 1919 to take control of the Detroit Museum of Art on behalf of the city of Detroit. Booth led the campaign to build the new museum, securing the services of the best professionals he could find: French émigré architect, Paul Philippe Cret, to design the building, and German émigré art historian, Dr. Wilhelm Valentiner, to direct the museum and develop the collection.

The Detroit Institute of Arts is a civic monument in white Vermont marble that relates to Cass Gilbert's Detroit Public Library across Woodward Avenue and reflects the principles of the City Beautiful movement of the turn of the century. It was designed by the Philadelphia architect Paul Philippe Cret. Born in France in 1876, Cret was trained at the Ecole des Beaux Arts, and his work is both rational and urbanely French. In this building the triple-arched entrance, the rhythmic windows, the low profile, and the curved entrance drive all signify his controlled approach. The galleries were arranged so that paintings could be displayed with sculpture and furniture in architectural settings that gave each room the same style as the art it contained. Dark gray, polished granite recent additions, which add gallery, research, and administrative space, contrast with and respect the dignified Cret Beaux-Arts Classical design by connecting themselves to the original building with bridges through existing window openings. The *Detroit Industry* mural devoted to the auto industry and painted by Diego Rivera in 1932–1933 is in Rivera Court.

66. Center for Creative Studies

William Kessler and Associates, 1972–1975

Resembling a Tinker Toy construction, this modular structural system of precast concrete components, with enlarged cylindrical columns designed to distribute mechanical and electrical utilities vertically, was built as art and music schools for the Detroit Society of Arts and Crafts and the Detroit Community Music School, the present-day Center for Creative Studies. It is located at 245 East Kirby Avenue.

The first exhibitions of handicrafts in Detroit in 1904 and 1905 precipitated the founding of the Detroit Society of Arts and Crafts in 1906. The society patterned itself after the tradition of William Morris for the purposes of reinstituting a standard of beauty in articles of everyday, practical use. The society sought to stimulate an interest in design and handicrafts and to provide a market for the crafts. George Gough Booth was a founding member, first president, and frequent patron of the artists whose works were displayed here. Other early members included architects Albert Kahn, H. J. Maxwell Grylls, Frank Baldwin, and William Buck Stratton; ceramist Mary Chase Perry Stratton and her collaborator, Horace James Caulkins; and artists Katherine and Alexandrine McEwen.

Center for Creative Studies, William Kessler and Associates, 1972-1975

The society's School Art Guild occupied, rented, and remodeled quarters until 1916, when it moved into a stuccoed Early English Cottage building at 47 Watson Street. Designed by members Stratton and Grylls, the building featured salesrooms, galleries, workshops, and a theater. The art school was replaced in 1958 with a glass-walled building surrounded by a brick screen wall embracing a courtyard, designed by Yamasaki, Leinweber and Associates and erected on East Kirby Avenue. Increasing student enrollment made this building inadequate, and, in 1920 Kessler began plans for a phased expansion. The present Center for Creative Studies relates to the brutalist architecture of Paul Rudolph's Endo Laboratories (1962–1964) in Garden City, New York. The Center for Creative Studies, and the complex as a whole, speaks of the importance of design in the Motor City.

67. Scarab Club *Lancelot Sukert, 1928–1929*

The Scarab Club, located at 217 Farnsworth Street, was established in 1916. Its purpose was "to promote the mutual acquaintance of art lovers and art workers, to stimulate and guide toward practical expression the artistic sense of the people of Detroit, and to advance the knowledge and love of the Fine Arts in every possible manner." Booth was among its members, who included painters, sculptors, architects, engravers, illustrators, musicians, and writers. The club's precursor was the Hopkin Club, which was founded in 1907 and named in honor of Detroit artist Robert Hopkin. Initially the Scarab Club occupied temporary quarters. In 1922, under the club president, Henry G. Stevens, the members selected a site adjacent to the art institute and began plans to build the present clubhouse. It is used for entertainment and social purposes and to provide studio and exhibition facilities for its artist members.

The plain brick building blends the Moderne with the Arts and Crafts. In the facade three groups of windows are recessed between flat piers over a band of zigzag brick and another row of terra cotta grilles. High above the entrance a medallion manufactured by the Pewabic Pottery, on which is represented the figure of a scarab in turquoise, green, and gold, distinctly marks the brick wall. The first-floor gallery opens to a courtyard on the north. Over the fireplace on the wooden beamed and paneled second-floor lounge, a mural painted by Paul Honore depicts the Scarab "family tree." Six well-lighted studios with galleries occupy the third floor. The club was designed by Lancelot Sukert, a Detroit architect who belonged to the Scarab Club. Sukert studied architecture at the Universities of California and Pennsylvania. Before starting his own office in 1921, he worked briefly in New York and in the office of Albert Kahn. Sukert explained that the Scarab Club building is "a composite of ideas contributed by many members." The clubhouse is important to the cultural life of Detroit

68. Pewabic Pottery *William B. Stratton, 1907*

In 1904 Mary Chase Perry founded the Pewabic Pottery Company, naming it after the Pewabic Copper Mine near her hometown of Hancock in the Upper Peninsula. In 1908 she moved her ceramic operation to its permanent studio, this English half-timber cottage designed by a prominent Detroit architect, William B. Stratton, whom she later married. Not only does the structure harken back to the English cottage in its design, with the steep medieval roof, it does so in its function as a house for the small industry. Located at 10125 East Jefferson Avenue, Pewabic Pottery became a central part of the Arts and Crafts movement in Detroit. In collaboration with Horace James Caulkins, a Detroit manufacturer of dental products, Perry systematically experimented with new firing techniques and chemical glazes in a revolutionary oil-burning kiln, which led her to the discovery of beautiful iridescent glazes. Architectural tiles fired by Mary Chase Stratton in the kilns of the Pewabic Pottery are found in many buildings at Cranbrook and in distinguished buildings throughout Michigan and the entire United States.

Pewabic Pottery

Mary Chase Perry Stratton laying Pewabic tile at Rainbow Spring, 1915–16, Cranbrook Archives

Bibliography

The history of Cranbrook cannot be understood without reference to the history, the fortunes, and conditions of the city of Detroit and the Arts and Crafts Movement.

Since Cranbrook is sponsoring a number of publications in connection with its Centennial celebration in 2004, and the anniversary itself will no doubt prompt many others, the following short and highly unsystematic list of books and articles will perforce be outdated almost from the moment of its publication. The reader is advised, in particular, to look forward to the completion of the videos on four recent construction projects and on the repair and restoration at Cranbrook by Marsha Miro.

Collections

All collections are in the Cranbrook Archives unless otherwise noted.

These include the most important collections for the study of Cranbrook architecture and history: Ellen Warren Scripps Booth; George Gough Booth; Henry Scripps and Carolyn Farr Booth; Christ Church Cranbrook; Cranbrook Academy of Art, Office of the Director, 1932–1990; Cranbrook Academy of Art, Organization Documents; Cranbrook Academy of Art Records, 1930–1998; Cranbrook Architectural Office Files, 1925–1987; Cranbrook Art Council Notebooks (Unprocessed); Cranbrook Educational Community, Assistant to the President Records, 1970–1989; Cranbrook Educational Community Board of Trustees Records, 1927–1995; Cranbrook Foundation Correspondence and Office Records Series, 1926–1973; Cranbrook House and Gardens Auxiliary Records, 1950–1995; Cranbrook Public Relations and Marketing Department,. 1990–1998; Samuel Simpson Marquis; Saarinen Family Papers, c. 1880–1889; William Oliver Stevens, 1927–1935; J. Robert F. and Pipsan Saarinen Swanson.

Architectural Drawings

Brook (Cranbrook Yearbook), 1931–1989;
Cranbrook Annual Report
Crane-Clarion
Cranbrook Art Academy. Graduate Studies. Bloomfield Hills: n.p, n.d.
Cranbrook House. Bloomfield Hills, Michigan: n.p., n.d.
Cranbrook House and Gardens Auxiliary. n.p., 1999.
Cranbrook Photograph File
Cranbrook School. Bloomfield Hills, n.p., n.d
Cranbrook Schools Brookside Lower School. n.p., n.d.
Detroit Publishing Company. Prints and Photographs Division, Library of Congress, Washington, D. C.
Woodwinds (Kingswood School Yearbook), 1932–1990.

Allen, Sanford H. *Comments on Accounts of The Cranbrook Foundation: A Guide to its Ledger Accounts.* [n.d. post-1958.]

Coir, Mark. *George Gough Booth and the Planning of Cranbrook.* Detroit. Wayne State University, Department of History. April 1992.

Coir, Mark. Notes on the Building of Christ Church Cranbrook. [n.d.]

DeFord, Carole S. Preliminary Land Use History: Cranbrook Homestead (3 May 3, 1991).

Elstein, Rochelle Berger. *Life and Career of Dankmar Adler (1844–1900).* 1995.

"Kingswood School Cranbrook: A Country Day and Boarding School for Girls." Announcement [n.p., n.d.].

Paulsen, Glen, and Associates, Architects. Cranbrook General Development Plan (May 5, 1966).

"Presentation Address by Mr. George G. Booth At the Cranbrook School Dedicatory Exercises, October 28, 1927."

"Values, Ideas and Form: Cranbrook and Architecture." [n.p., n.d.].

Secondary Sources

"Ampliamento della Brookside School a Cranbrook." *Casabella* 644 (April 1997): 20–27.

Balmori, Diane. "Cranbrook: The Invisible Landscape." *Journal of the Society of Architectural Historians* 53, no. 1 (March 1994): 30–60.

Bailey, Anson. "The Home of Eliel Saarinen at the Cranbrook Academy of Art." *The Master Builder* (August 1934): 231–236.

Benson, Robert. "A Sense of Cranbrook: The Brookside Kindergarten." *Inland Architect* (September–October 1987): 64–65.

———. "The Cranbrook Community Examines its Future." *Inland Architect* (September–October 1987): 53–63.

Boles, Daralice Donkervoet. "Albert Kahn." Placzek, Adolf K., ed. *Macmillan Encyclopedia of Architects.* New York: Free Press, 1982

Booth, Charles, and Mark Coir. *Booth Family* [video]. Bloomfield Hills, Michigan, 1999.

Booth, Henry S. *Pilgrims's Guide to Christ Church Cranbrook.* [n.p., n.d.]

Brock, H. I. "Old-World Wood Carver Practices his Art Here." *New York Times Magazine* (March 28, 1926): 6.

Burke, Janet, ed. *The Cranbrook Vision: A Community Perspective.* Bloomfield Hills, Michigan: Cranbrook Educational Community, n.d. [circa 1986]

Burroughs, Clyde H. "The Greek Theater at Bloomfield Hills, Michigan." *Art and Archaeology* (March 1917): 172–179.

"Burrowes, Marcus R., Obituary." *Detroit Free Press* (July 18, 1953).

Brookside School Cranbrook: A School for Young Children. Bloomfield Hills, Michigan: [n.d.]

Carson, Ray. "Entrance, Arrival Features Unveiled." *Cranbrook Journal* (Winter 1994): 3.

Cheney, Sheldon. "Designing the Open-Air Theatre." *American Architect* 116, no. 2297 (December 31, 1919): 803–810.

Christ-Janer, Albert. *Eliel Saarinen: Finnish-American Architect and Educator.* Chicago and London: University of Chicago Press, 1979.

Clark, Robert Judson, et al. *Design in America: The Cranbrook Vision 1925–1950.* New York: Harry N. Abrams, Inc., 1983.

Coir, Mark. "Morris Mill: The Flow of History at Cranbrook." *Cranbrook-Kingswood Tradition* (Winter 1993): 14–15.

Colby, Joy Hakanson. *Art and a City: A History of the Detroit Society of Arts & Crafts.* Detroit: Wayne State University Press, 1956.

Comara, Mary. "Historic Architecture: Eliel Saarinen." *Architectural Digest* 38, no. 1 (January 1981): 130–136.

Coulter, Bruce Noel. *Forty Years On: A History of Cranbrook School, Bloomfield Hills, Michigan.* Bloomfield Hills, Michigan: Cranbrook School, 1976.

Cranbrook: Evolution of a Dream. Bloomfield Hills, Michigan: Cranbrook Educational Community, c. 1997.

"Cranbrook School, Bloomfield Hills, Michigan: Eliel Saarinen, Architect." *Architectural Record* 64, no. 6 (December 1928): 452–460, 476–505, 525–528.

Davies, Florence. "Christ Church, Cranbrook: A Work of Art in which Artists, Craftsmen and Artisans Collaborated." *American Magazine of Art* 20, no. 6 (June 1929): 311–325.

———. "The Weavings of Loja Saarinen." *The Weaver* (January 1937): 13–17, 31.

———. "Cranbrook." *American Magazine of Art* 18, no. 8 (August 1927): 403–413.

Derbabian, Anahid Lisa. "A Freestyle Design." *Cranbrook Journal* (Winter–Spring 1998): 2–7.

Detroit Institute of Arts. *Arts and Crafts in Detroit 1906–1976; The Movement, the Society, the School.* Detroit: Detroit Institute of Arts, c. 1976.

Dunlap, David W. "A Modern Master's Spirit Soars Anew." *New York Times* (June 3, 1999): B14.

"Eero Saarinen." *Monthly Bulletin Michigan Society of Architects* 53, no.10 (October 1961):11–13.

Erickson, Annmarie. "A Gentle Fortress." *Cranbrook Journal* (Spring 1995): 2–7.

———. "Juggling Oranges in the Air." *Cranbrook Journal* (Winter–Spring 1998): 8–11.

———. "The New Institute: A Place of Wonder." *Cranbrook Journal* (Summer 1996): 2–9.

Filler, Martin. "Where the Teacher is Beauty." *House & Garden* 154, no. 4 (April 1982): 112–117, 170.

Fox, Jean M. *Marcus Burrowes (1874–1953), English Revival Architect.* Farmington Hills, Michigan, 1992.

Frampton, Kenneth. "Cranbrook After Saarinen." *Architecture* (March 1999): 75–89.

Frayer, William A. "Education Through Environment." *The Nation's Schools* (February 1936): 18–22.

Gerard, John. *A Quiet Grandeur: The Architectural Drawings of Eliel Saarinen for Kingswood School Cranbrook.* Bloomfield Hills, Michigan: Cranbrook Academy of Art Museum, 1984.

Goldberger, Paul. "The Cranbrook Vision," *New York Times Magazine* Section 6 (April 8, 1984): 56.

Goldberger, Paul. "A Treasurehouse for Architecture." *New York Times* (May 7, 1989).

Grese, Robert E. "Ossian Cole Simonds." Tishler, William H., ed. *American Landscape Architecture: Designers and Places.* Washington, D. C., Preservation Press, 1989.

Halik, Nancy Lickerman. "The Eero Saarinen Spawn." *Inland Architect* 25, no. 4 (May 1981): 14–43.

Hamlin, Talbot Faulkner. "The Prize-Winning Buildings of 1931." *Architectural Record* 71, no. 1 (January 1932): 11.

Hawthorne, Ella Mae. "Cranbrook, Mr. Booth's Estate Near Detroit." *Town and Country* (August 24, 1912): 20–21.

Hay, Jessica Ayer. "The Story of the Two Artists Who Are Designing Cranbrook School." *Afterglow* 3, no. 9 (September 1927): 5, 15–17.

Hildebrand, Grant. *Designing for Industry: The Architecture of Albert Kahn*. Cambridge, Massachusetts, and London, England: Massachusetts Institute of Technology, 1974.

Hoffman, Dan. *Architecture Studio: Cranbrook Academy of Art*. New York: Rizzoli, 1994.

Holl, Steven. "Architettura e Progrette: Ristrutturazione e ampliamento del Cranbrook Institute of Science." *Casabella* 2011, no. 644 (April 1997): 28–35.

Ingersoll, Richard. "Between Typology and Fetish." *Architecture* (March 1999): 80–89.

Iorio, Mary E. "Triton's Return." *Cranbrook Journal* (Winter–Spring 1998): 31.

Jenkin, Denise. "Whole New World at Cranbrook." *Oakland Press* (August 7, 1996): A10.

Kaplan, Richard. "The Economics of Popular Journalism in the Gilded Age: Detroit *Evening News* in 1873 and 1888." *Journalism History* 21, no. 2 (Summer 1995): 65–78.

Kimmelman, Michael. "The Cranbrook Vision." *Connoisseur* 213, no. 854 (April 1983): 31–36.

King, R. J. "Cranbrook Looks to Past to Prepare Students for Future." *Detroit News* (March 2,1997).

"The Kingswood School for Girls, Cranbrook, Michigan, Eliel Saarinen, Architect." *Architectural Forum* (January 1932): 32–60.

Louchheim, Aline B. "Now Saarinen the Son." *New York Times Magazine* Section 6 (April 26, 1953): 26–27, 44 45.

Marquis, Albert Nelson, ed. *Book of Detroiters*. Chicago: A.N. Marquis & Company, 1908.

McMechan, Jervis Bell. *Christ Church Cranbrook*. Bloomfield Hill, Michigan: Christ Church Cranbrook, 1979.

Miller, R. Craig. "Eliel Saarinen" and "Eero Saarinen." Placzek, Adolf K., ed. *Macmillan Encyclopedia of Architects*. New York: Free Press, 1982.

Millington, Theodore H. "A Trip to Cranbrook Estate, Church and School." *Afterglow* 3, no. 9 (September 1927): 2–4, 27–28.

Miro, Marsha. *Cranbrook: Evolution of a Dream*, 4 volumes [video]. Detroit/Troy [TK] Sue Marx Films, Inc. 1997–2000.

———. "Design as Discourse: La scuola di Cranbrook." *Casabella* 646 (June 1997): 38–47.

———. "Finishing School." *Cranbrook Journal* (Fall–Winter 1998): 10–12.

———. *A History of Cranbrook*. Bloomfield Hills, Cranbrook Art Museum, forthcoming 2000.

Miro, Marsha and Mark Coir. "Architettura e Progetti: Il sogno di Cranbrook." *Casabella* 644 (April 1997): 2–19.

Miro, Marsha and Dan Hoffman, ed. *New Construction at Cranbrook*. 4 vols (video). Forthcoming, 2004.

"Modern Hellenism." *Art and Artists: A Monthly Magazine of All the Arts* 1, no. 4 (August 1916): 3–7, 11.

"Museum and Library, Cranbrook Academy of Art, Bloomfield Hills, Mich.: Eliel Saarinen, Architect." *Pencil Points* (December 1943): 36–49.

Oliver, Richard. "Bertram Grosvenor Goodhue." Placzek, Adolf K., ed. *MacMillan Encyclopedia of Architects*. New York: Free Press, 1982.

Pear, Lillian Myers. *The Pewabic Pottery: A History of Its Products and Its People*. Des Moines, Iowa: Wallace-Homestead Book Company, 1976.

Pound, Arthur. *The Only Thing Worth Finding: The Life and Legacies of George Gough Booth*. Detroit: Wayne State University Press, 1964.

"Publishers' Department." *The Architectural Review* ( ): xi [TK on this source]

Reid, Kenneth. "Eliel Saarinen—Master of Design." *Pencil Points* 17 (September 1936): 464–494.

Roberts, Eileen L. "Ionic Order Restored." *Inland Architect* 35, no. 4 (July–August 1991): 21–22, 25.

———. "Replicas of Italian Medieval Sculpture at Cranbrook: A Chapter in the History of American Taste." *Source: Notes in the History of Art* 9, no. 4 (Summer 1990): 22–29.

Rose, Judy. "Cranbrook to Get More Science." *Detroit Free Press* (August 7, 1996).

Rose, Peter. "Ampliamento della Brookside School a Cranbrook." *Casabella* 644 (April 1997): 20–27.

———. *Cranbrook Journal.* (Spring 1995): back cover.

Rutz, Miriam E. "The Cranbrook Garden: Home of George and Ellen Booth." *Chronicle (The Quarterly Magazine of the Historical Society of Michigan)* 25, no. 4 (Spring 1990): 1–3.

S. O. H. "The Masque of Arcadia or the Finding of the Blue Rose." *Handcraft* 3 (1910): 208.

Sandler, Linda. "Reading, Writing and Borrowing: Famed Cranbrook School and Others Turn to Wall Street." *Wall Street Journal* (May 6, 1998): B8.

Snyder, Ben M., III. *"Once More With Joy": Perspectives of Cranbrook School for Boys.* Bloomfield Hills, Michigan: Cranbrook Press, 1997.

Stein, Karen D. "Magnificent Obsession: Portfolio." *Architectural Record* 175, no. 11 (mid-September 1987): 90.

Stevens, Thomas Wood. "American Pageant Parent Praises Greek Theatre and the Masque at Cranbrook." *(Detroit) News Tribune* (July 16, 1916).

Stevens, William O. "The Arts in Cranbrook School." *The Fine Arts Forecast* 2, no. 2 (October 1929): 22.

Sullivan, Louis. "The Chicago Tribune Competition," *Architectural Record* 53 (February 1923): 152–53.

Temko, Allan. *Eero Saarinen.* New York: George Braziller, 1962.

Thistle [Henry Scripps Booth]. *The Gardens and Park of Cranbrook House.* Bloomfield Hills, Michigan: Cranbrook Press, 1951.

Tilghman, Donnell. "Eliel Saarinen." *Architectural Record* 63, no. 5 (May 1928): 393–402.

United States Department of the Interior, National Park Service, National Register of Historic Places Registration Form. "Cranbrook." Prepared by Carolyn Pitts, February 9, 1989.

———. National Register of Historic Places Registration Form. "William B. and Mary Shuford Palmer House." Prepared by Kathryn Bishop Eckert, 1998. [TK: should the above two items be listed in the unpublished sources section above??]

Venturi, Robert, Denise Scott Brown and Steven Izenour. *Learning from Las Vegas.* Cambridge, Massachusetts, and London, England: MIT Press, 1972.

Verneuil, M. P. *Carl Milles: Sculpteur Suedois.* Paris et Bruxelles, 1929.

Von Eckardt, Wolf. "Cranbrook's Glorious First Half Century." *Architecture* 72, no. 9 (September 1983): 50–57.

Welch, Jeffrey. "Cranbrook's Signature Space." *Cranbrook Journal* (Winter–Spring 1998): 28–30.

White, Lee A., Robert T. Hatt, and others. *Cranbrook Institute of Science: A History of its Founding and First Twenty-Five Years.* Bloomfield Hills, Michigan: Cranbrook Institute of Science, 1959.

White, Lee. *The Detroit News: 1873-1917.* Detroit: Evening News Association, 1918.

Wittkopp, Gregory, ed. *Saarinen House and Garden: a Total Work of Art.* New York: Harry N. Abrams, 1995.

Walk One

Hawthorne, Ella Mae. "Cranbrook, Mr. Booth's Estate Near Detroit." *Town and Country* (August 24, 1912): 20–21.

Kaplan, Richard. "The Economics of Popular Journalism in the Gilded Age: The Detroit *Evening News* in 1873 and 1888." *Journalism History* 21, no. 2 (Summer 1995): 65–78.

Walk Two

Jessie Winter to Mr. and Mrs. Booth, May 11, 1932. George Gough Booth Papers, Cranbrook Archives.

Cranbrook Journal (Spring 1995). [Peter Rose, architect, photograph on back cover.]

Walk Three

George Booth to the Reverend Samuel Simpson Marquis, D.D., October 4, 1923, George Gough Booth Papers, Cranbrook Archives.

Katherine McEwen to George Booth, September 9 and November 6, 1926, George Gough Booth Papers, Cranbrook Archives.

McEwen, Katherine. *Design for the Decoration of the Chancel*, n.d. [probably 1925].

McMechan, Jervis Bell. *Christ Church Cranbrook*. Bloomfield Hill, Michigan: Christ Church Cranbrook, 1979.

Walk Four

Booth, George Gough. "Memorandum on the Founding of Cranbrook School." January 12, 1937. George Gough Booth Papers, Cranbrook Archives.

George Booth to G. Owen Bonawit, July 23, 1928. George Gough Booth Papers, Cranbrook Archives.

George Booth to Swedish Arts and Crafts Company, Chicago, June 4, 1928. George Gough Booth Papers, Cranbrook Archives.

George Booth to Oscar B. Bach, January 10, 1927. George Gough Booth Papers, Cranbrook Archives.

Trust Indenture Explanatory Statement, November 1, 1927. Cranbrook Archives.

Walk Five

Booth, George Gough. *An Academy of Art at Cranbrook*, 1925. George Gough Booth Papers, Cranbrook Archives.

Coir, Mark. *George Gough Booth and the Planning of Cranbrook*. Wayne State University, Department of History, 1992. Cranbrook Archives.

Filler, Martin. "Where the Teacher is Beauty." *House & Garden* 154, no. 4 (April 1982): 112.

George Gough Booth. Notes, October 1924. George Gough Booth Papers, Cranbrook Archives.

George Booth to Eliel Saarinen, October 6, 1924. Cranbrook Archives.

Minutes of the Cranbrook Art Council, 1933–1934. Cranbrook Archives.

Saarinen, Eliel. "Analysis of Past and Future Educational Policies of the Cranbrook Academy of Art, July 12, 1942. George Gough Booth Papers, Cranbrook Archives.

Saarinen, Eliel. "The Story of Cranbrook." Saarinen Family Papers, c. 1950, Cranbrook Archives.

Walk Six

Agreement between the Cranbrook Foundation and the Trustees. July 24, 1930. Cranbrook Foundation Records, Cranbrook Archives.

Booth, George Gough. "Memoranda for the consideration of the Board of Trustees provided for in my Will for the administration of the Estate of Cranbrook as an educational centre." January 15, 1927 (first written December 1926). Cranbrook Archives.

Edward A. Eichstaedt to George Booth, April 21, 1934. George Gough Booth Papers, Cranbrook Archives.

Filler, Martin. "Where the Teacher is Beauty." *House & Garden* 154, no. 4 (April 1982).

Walk Seven

Erickson, Annmarie. "The New Institute: A Place of Wonder." *Cranbrook Journal* (Summer 1996): 2–9.

Holl, Steven. "Architettura e Progetti: Ristrutturazione e ampliamento del Cranbrook Institute of Science." *Casabella* 2011, no. 644 (April 1997): 28–35.

Saarinen, Eliel. "The Story of Cranbrook," and "Cranbrook." (c. 1950.) Cranbrook Archives.

Stein, Karen D. "Magnificent Obsession." *Architectural Record* 175, no. 11 (mid-September 1987): 90.

White, Lee A. and Robert T. Hatt and others. *Cranbrook Institute of Science: A History of its Founding and First Twenty-Five Years.* Bloomfiled Hills, Michigan: Cranbrook Institute of Science, 1959. [Deed of Trust, February 10, 1932.]

Walk Eight

Louchheim, Aline B. "Now Saarinen the Son." *New York Times Magazine* Section 6 (April 26, 1953): 26.

Eero Saarinen to George Gough Booth, January 2, 1942. George Gough Booth Papers, Cranbrook Archives.

Walk Nine

White, Lee A. *The Detroit News: 1873–1917.* Detroit: The Evening News Association, 1918.

[Artist, title, date, medium, location]

Aaltonen, Waino. *Kivi's Muse* (from the *Alexksis Kivi Monument*), designed 1926, cast 1930, bronze, Cranbrook Academy of Art: Saarinen House courtyard.

Chinese. *Sacred Lion Dog*, fifth to sixth century, marble, 32 × 27 × 31½ in., Cranbrook Art Museum: East Stairs (Ramp).

Anonymous. *Quadrangle Fountain* (replica of the fountain in cloister of Monreale Cathedral, Palermo, Sicily, installed in base and pool designed by Eliel Saarinen), 1927, marble, Cranbrook School: Quadrangle.

Anonymous. *The Wrestlers,* twentieth-century copy of fourth-century B.C. original, by student of Lysippus, bronze, Cranbrook School, Alumni Court.

Bach, Oscar Bruno. *Clock of the Handicrafts (Craftsmen Clock),* 1927, bronze and wrought iron, Cranbrook School: Dining Hall.

Bissell, George Edwin. *Diogenes*, 1906, bronze, 24 in., Cranbrook School: Tower.

Bonawit, G. Owen. *Christopher Columbus Window*, 1927, stained glass, Cranbrook School: Hoey Hall, Upper Assembly Lobby.

Bonawit, G. Owen. Old Printers Marks of Galliot Du Pré and Jacob Stadelberger, circa 1928, stained glass, Cranbrook School, Library.

d'Ascenzo, Nicola. *Scenes from the Life of Christ Window*, 1927, stained glass, Christ Church: East Window.

Dearle, J. H., (executed by Tapestry Works of Morris and Company, Merton Abbey, England). *Old Dispensation or Rule of Law, and New Dispensation or Rule of Love Tapestries*, 1925–1932, dyed wools, Christ Church: Narthex.

Evans, David. *Cranbrook School Football Team*, 1930, bronze, Cranbrook School: Thompson Oval and Stadium.

Fredericks, Marshall M. *Persephone, Goddess of Spring,* 1965, bronze, Homestead Properties: Greek Theatre, Pool.

Fredericks, Marshall M. *Two Sisters,* 1965, bronze, 72 in., Kingswood School: Alumnae Court.

Friedlander, Leo, Edward F. Caldwell and Company, Inc., executed the base with Victor F. von Lossberg of E. F. Caldwell & Co., designer. *Baptismal Font*, by 1928, copper and enamel-on-brass cover and marble base, Christ Church: Chapel of Saint John.

Herter, Albert. *The Great Crusade*, 1920, tapestry woven on cotton warps with wool, silk, metal threads (gold) and mercerized cotton, Homestead Properties: Cranbrook House, Library.

Hession, John, Jr.,. *Map of North America Depicting the Principle Expeditions of Discovery and Exploration* , 1928, watercolor and egg tempera, Cranbrook School: Hoey Hall, North Entrance Lobby.

Hogan, James H., for James Powell & Sons (Whitefriars) Ltd., London. *Womankind Window*, 1927, painted antique glass, Christ Church: West Window.

Kerr, Peter. *Aim High*, 1972, bronze, Cranbrook School: Quadrangle.

Kirchmayer, John. Relief carving from sketch by George Gough Booth. *Overmantel*, 1918, wood, Homestead Properties: Cranbrook House, Library.

Manship, Paul. *Armillary Sphere*, c.1924, bronze, Cranbrook School: Quadrangle.

Mantynen, Jussi. *Pair of Lynx with Their Young*, c. 1935, black granite, Cranbrook Art Museum: Front (North) Stairs.

Maroti, Geza. *Galileo Portal*, 1928, relief sculpture, limestone, Cranbrook School: Hoey Hall, Lower Level or Science Door Entrance.

Maroti, Geza. *The Gift of Knowledge*, 1927–1928, chimneypiece relief sculpture, limestone, Cranbrook School: Library.

Maroti, Geza. *Knowledge*, 1928, entrance decoration, wood, Cranbrook School: Junior Study Hall.

McEwen, Katherine. *Church's Foundation*, 1925–1928, fresco, Christ Church: Chancel.

Mc Vey, William. *Birds in Flight*, 1952–53, bronze, Brookside School.

Milles, Carl. *Dancing Girls,* c. 1912–1913, bronze, Kingswood: North Shore of Lake.

Milles, Carl. *Diana*, c. 1928, bronze, Kingswood: North Court.

Milles, Carl. *Europa and the Bull,* designed c. 1915–1916, cast 1935, bronze, Cranbrook Art Museum and Library: Triton Pool, North Center.

Milles, Carl. *Folke Filbyter on a Horse* (reduction of central figure of the Folkunga fountain in Linkoping), bronze, c. 1924, Cranbrook Art Museum: Propylaeum.

Milles, Carl. *Jonah and the Whale* Fountain, 1932, bronze, 108 × 124 in. (height × diameter), Academy Way (currently offsite for conservation), Gift of the Cranbrook Foundation.

Milles, Carl. *Mermaids and Tritons*, three sculptures, designed c. 1925–1927, cast c. 1925–1934, bronze, various dimensions, Cranbrook Institute of Science: Pool.

Milles, Carl. *Orpheus* Fountain (regrouping of eight figures from Orpheus Fountain for the Concert Hall, Stockholm, Sweden), cast 1937, bronze, Cranbrook Art Museum: Quadrangle (North).

Milles, Carl. *Pair of Running Boars* (made for courtyard of Swedish Match Company Building), designed c. 1925, cast c. 1925–1934, bronze, Cranbrook Institute of Science: Old Entrance.

Milles, Carl. *Pair of Running Deer* (original design made for courtyard of Swedish Match company Building), c. 1925, bronze, Arts and Crafts Courtyard Stairs.

Milles, Carl. *Running Dogs (Coursing Hounds)* (made at Lidingo, Sweden, at request of Lord Melchett of England), c. 1910s–1934, bronze, Cranbrook School: East Stairs.

Milles, Carl. *Pair of Wild Boars* (originals made at Lidingo, Sweden, c. 1926 for Lord Melchett's Castle, England), designed c. 1926, cast c. 1929, bronze, Cranbrook Academy of Art: Nichols Gate.

Milles, Carl. *Siren with Fishes,* designed 1916–1918, cast 1935, bronze, Cranbrook Art Academy: West of Academy Way.

Milles, Carl. *Sunglitter (Naiad and Dolphin)* (duplicate at National Museum, Sweden), c. 1917–1918, bronze, Cranbrook Academy of Art: Arts and Crafts Courtyard, top of stairs.

Milles, Carl. *Sven Hedin on a Camel*, c. 1910s–1934, bronze, Cranbrook Institute of Science: South of Original Entrance.

Milles, Carl. *Robert E. Lee Group (Teachers of Youth)*, early twentieth century, bronze, Cranbrook School: James C. Gordon Hall of Science.

Milles, Carl. *Triton* Pool, designed early twentieth century, cast 1930s, bronze, Cranbrook Academy of Art, Triton Pool.

Della Porta, Giacomo (Jacobo) (designer); Landini, Taddeo (sculptor). *Turtle Fountain* (replica of the Fontana della Tartarughe of Rome, sixteenth century, installed 1924, restored 1981, Homestead Properties: Cranbrook House, North Terrace.

Saarinen, Eliel, and Bach, Oscar Bruno. *Main Entrance Gate (Peacock Gate)*, 1927, wrought iron, Cranbrook School.

Saarinen, Eliel (fabricated by Walter Nichols). *Nichols Gate*, 1941, wrought-iron, Cranbrook Academy of Art.

Saarinen, Eliel (possibly fabricated by Walter Nichols or by John Burnitt). *Kingswood Main Gates,* c. 1932, wrought iron, Kingswood School.

Saarinen, Loja. *Festival of the May Queen* tapestry, 1932, coarse homespun linen and wool, Kingswood School: Dining Room.

Yellin, Samuel. *Main Entrance Gates*, 1917, wrought iron, Homestead Properties: Cranbrook House, 380 Lone Pine Road.

Acknowledgments

I would like to thank Ray Carson, Director of Public Relations, Cranbrook Educational Community, and Mark Coir, Cranbrook Archivist, who thoughtfully reviewed the draft manuscript and offered comments that greatly improved the work.

Mark Coir directed me to the extensive institution and architectural records of the Cranbrook Archives and told me many interesting stories about the Booths and Cranbrook. Cathy Price, Amy James, Ryan Wieber, Marsha Miro, Cora Joyce Rauss of the Cranbrook Archives guided me through the holdings of the archives. Roberta Gilboe, Registrar, Art Museum, Cranbrook Art Academy, and Robert Saarnio, Curator of Cultural Properties, conducted research on the art works cited in the Checklist of Significant Works of Art Discussed in *Cranbrook Campus* to verify facts. Ed Thompson presented a session on the hydrology of the campus. Jean Claude Asar discussed the forthcoming studios addition to Cranbrook Academy of Art. Patty Shea of the Cranbrook House and Gardens Auxiliary described the gardens and the amazing work of auxiliary volunteers. Thanks especially to Rae Dumke and Lynn Merrill-Francis of the Michigan AIA, who suggested I write this guide.

(*Italics* indicates a photograph.)

A. H. Davenport Company, 63
Aalto, Alvar, 13, 117
Aaltonen, Vaino, 107
Academic Building. *See* Hoey Hall
Academy Quadrangle, *94–95, 120*–21
Academy Way, 2, 12, 96, 99, 104–5, 108, 111–12, 142–43
Academy Way Houses, 94–95, 112
Academy Way Studios, 94–95, 112
Adams, Katherine Rogers, 126
Aim High (sculpture), 76
Albert and Ernestine Krolik Kahn House, *168*
Alexis Rudier Fondeur (France), 77
Alumnae Court, 137
Alumni Court, *68–69, 75, 77, 81*
American Federation of Arts, 97
American Institute of Architects (AIA), 46
 award to Eero Saarinen, 156
 Michigan chapter, 19
 New York chapter
  award for Cranbrook Institute of Science, 147
Andersson-Wirde, Maja, *101,* 130
Angley Woods, 124
Architectural League of New York
 award for Christ Church Cranbrook, 60
 award to Saarinen, 72
Architectural Record, 10n, 147
Ardolino, Edward, 60
Armillary Sphere, 76
art, 1, 7, 15, 76, 96–103
 See also under Cranbrook Academy of Art and Museum
Art Academy/Administration Building, 37, *94–95,* 101, *103–4,* 111
Art Alliance of America, 97
Art Club, 101, 105, 112
Art Deco style, vii, 108
Arts and Crafts, School of, 6, 100
Arts and Crafts Building, *94–95,* 100–1, *105*
Arts and Crafts movement, vii, 1, 5, 20, 24, 26–27, 32, 36–37, 40, 42, 56, 62, 72, 88, 96–98, 110, 164, 171–72
Assembly Hall, 79
 See also under Hoey Hall
Augur, Margaret, 126–27
Auto Court, 76

Bach, Oscar Bruno, 64, 74, 88
Bagley, Amasa, 35
Bagley's Corners. *See* Bloomfield Center
Baldwin, Frank, 171
Barbour, Margaret Chittenden, 40
Barbour, William T., 40
Barnes, Edward Larrabee, 13
Bassett, Charles, 157
Batik Department, 100
Bauder, Lillian, 8, 146
Beresford, Florence Louise Booth, 60, 145, 158
Beresford, James Alfred, 60, 145, 158
Berglund, Tor, 100, 105, 108
Bertoia, Harry, 101. 103
Billington, Cecil, 140
Birkerts, Gunnar, 117, 157, 170
Birmingham, Michigan, 58, 73, 158
 City Hall and Library, *152–53, 159*
Bissell, George Edwin, 79

Black, Palmer, 111
Bloomfield Center, 35
Bloomfield Flouring Mill. *See* Mill House
Bloomfield Hills, Michigan, 1, 18, 20–21, 40–41, 58, 60, 73, 99, 124, 126, *152–53,* 154, 157
 as historic district, 155
Bloomfield Hills School, 40–41, 54
Bloomfield Hills Seminary, 40, 154
Bloomfield Hills Township, 3, 40, 156
boathouse. *See* Italian Boathouse
Bog Garden, 22
Bonawit, G. Owen, 60, *63,* 79–80
Book Bindery Department, 100, 105
Booth, Alice Newcomb, 158
Booth, Carolyn Farr, 36, 60, 158
Booth, Clara Louise Irene Gagnier, 5, 18, 28, 58
Booth, Edmund Wood, 18
Booth, Ellen (Nellie) Warren Scripps, vii, ix, *1–3,* 5–6, 8, 18–22, 28, 40–41, 43, 49, 54, 66, 73, 77, 114 15, 124 27, 129, 137, 154, 158, 164
Booth, Florence Louise, 20–21
Booth, George Coleman, 37
Booth, George Gough, vii, ix, *1–3,* 5–6, 8–9, 18–22, 24, 26–28, 30, 37, 40–44, 49, 54–55, 77, 80, 93, 111, 114–15, 121, 124–27, 129, 133, 137, 154–55, 157–58, 164, 166, 170
 and Christ Church Cranbrook, 54–58, 62–64, 66
 and Cranbrook Academy of Art, 96–102
 and Cranbrook Institute of Science, 140–43
 and Cranbrook schools, 70–71, 73, 86
  dedicatory remarks, 73
 honorary membership, American Institute of Architects (Michigan), 19
 and Kingswood School, 124–27, 129, 137
Booth, Grace Ellen, 20
Booth, Henry Scripps, 5–6, 11, 20, 22, 29–30, 33, 36, 42, 44, 47, 51, 55, 60, 70, 79, 97, 99, 111, 124–25, 158
Booth, Henry Wood, 5, 18, 28, 34, 42, 54, 58
Booth, James Scripps, 6, 20, 29, 64, 99, 115
Booth, Jean McLaughlin, 29, 64
Booth, John McLaughlin, 29
Booth, Ralph Harman, 18, 170
Booth, Warren Scripps, 6, 20, 99, 158
Booth House (Cranbrook), *2*
 See also under Cranbrook House and Gardens
Booth house (Detroit), 19, 24
Booth News, Inc., 18
Booth Newspapers, Inc., 8
Bradford, Francis Scott, 62
Brady Lane, 36
Breuer, Marcel, 156
Bromley, Frank, 40
Bromley, Kate Agnes Thompson, 40
Brook, The, 74
Brookside House, *38–39, 51*
Brookside School, viii, 1, 5, 7–8, 40–46, *47–49,* 54, 97, 100, 124, 126
 New Wing of, 9, *38–39,* 40, 44–*46, 47–50*
Burnett, John C., 88, 90
Burrowes, Marcus R., *4–5,* 30, 37, 70, 159
Burrowes and Wells, 28–30, 106

Cabinet Shop, 100, 105
Cahalane, Victor H., 142

Caldwell, Edward F., and Company, 62
Carl Emil Anderson and Olga Granner Milles House, *94–95*, 106, 108, *110*–11
Carriage House, *16–17*, 29–30
Caulkins, Horace James, 171, 173
Cavanaugh, Jerome P., 170
Center for Creative Studies, 97*162–63, 171*–72
Children's School Trust, 41
Chinese Lion Dog (sculptures), *121*
Christ Church Cranbrook, 2, 5–6, *52–53*, 54–56, *57–59*, 60–*61*, 62, *63–65*, 66, 70–71, 100
   carillon, 65–66
   chapels, *58–59*, 60, 62, 64
   nave, *65*
   rectory, *52–53*, 57, 60, *66*
   sexton's house, *52–53*, 57, 60, *67*
   west façade, *57*
Clock of the Handicrafts, The, 88
Coir, Mark, 10n
Colonial Revival style, 92
Columbus Window, 79
Comstock, William, 101
conduct, code of, 74
Connections Theater, 150
Copeland, Elizabeth, 24
Corfield, H. J., 3, 24
Crafts Court. *See* Maija Grotel Court
Cram, Ralph Adams, 54–55, 169
Cranbrook
   Booths' move to, 1908, 19–20, 154
   buildings and grounds
      hours open to public, vi
   centennial, 2004, 8
   combining of institutions of, 6–7
   design movements antecedent to, 1
   as National Historic Landmark, vii, 9
   origin of name, 3, 74
   preservationist role of, 9–10, 12
   president's overview of, vii–ix
   purposes of, 7, 73, 86–87, 141–42
   relation to Christ Church Cranbrook, 54–56
   siting of component institutions, 1–2
   "The Great Restoration" campaign, 75
Cranbrook Academy of Art, vii, 1–2, 5–7, 9, 12–14, 21, 37, 72, 86, *94–95, 96–101*, 102–3, 111, 125, 157, 160
   ceremonial entrance, *114*
   Museum and Library, 114, *115–17*
      aerial views, *115*, 118
      Booth collections, books and art, 114–15
   planning for, 96–101
   purposes of, 96, 98, 102–3
   Studio Addition, 117–*18*
Cranbrook Architectural Advisory Council, 46
Cranbrook Architectural Office, 13, 29–30, 37, 45, 47, 50, 70, 90–92, 97, 99, 103–4, 112, 128, 140, 150
Cranbrook Archives, *16–17*, 36
Cranbrook Boys' Middle School Campus, *68–69, 93*
Cranbrook Educational Community, 8–9, 22, 56, 141–42
   organization of, 6–7
Cranbrook Farm No. 2, *4*
Cranbrook Foundation, 6–7, 22, 37, 41, 45, 99–102, 104, 111, 124–26, 140, 155
Cranbrook House and Gardens, 2, 8–9, 12, *16–17*, 20, 22–23, *24–29*, 142
   Auxiliary, 22–23, 28, 33–34, 151
      Holiday Tables, 22–23
      wildflower sale, 29
   Entrance Court, *25*

entrance gates, *24*
West Terrace, 96–97, 121
Cranbrook Institute of Science, 2, 5, 7–9, 11–13, 21, 29, 125, *138–39*, 140–*43, 144–46, 147–48, 149–51*
   Hall of Man, 142
   Hall of Minerals, 142
   Light Pylon, *143–44, 148*, 151
   New Wing, *138–39*, 145–*49*, 150
      Light Laboratory, 149, 151
   Pohndorf Collection (minerals), 141
   purposes of, 141
   Reflecting Pool, 143, *145*
   Skillman Wing for Physical Sciences, *143–45*
Cranbrook Kingswood Middle School, 7
Cranbrook Kingswood Upper School, 7, 73, 124, 127
   formation by merger of boys and girls schools, 7, 73
   Kingswood Campus, 124–*25*, 126–*27*
      Gate Lodge, 128
      Green Lobby, 130
      Kingswood School Building, 128–30, *131–32*, 133–*34*
      main entrance gate, *127*
      Oval Turning Circle, 127–*28*
      Wenger Gymnasium, *135–36*, 137
Cranbrook Press, 1, 55
Cranbrook Road, 1–2, 5, 11, 19, 40, 44, 49, 54, 56
Cranbrook School, 1, 5, 12, 22, 41, 45, 70–91, 97, 100, 103, 106, 111, 125
   Quadrangle, *68–69, 75–76, 86–87*
Cranbrook School Football (relief sculpture), 82
Cranbrook School for Boys, vii, *4–5*, 7, 73
Cranbrook Vision, The: A Community Perspective, 8, 117, 140, 146
Crane, The, 74
Crane Brook (England)
   Cranbrook name derived from, 74
Cranebrook School Quadrangle, 9, *68–69, 75–76, 86–87*
Cret, Paul Philippe, 170–71
Crossings (firm), 45

Dancing Girls (sculpture), *35*
d'Ascenzo, Nicola, 60, 64
De Salle, Albert, 114
De Salle, Peggy, 114
De Salle Auditorium, *94–95*, 114, 117
Dearle, J. H., 63
Death of Wolfe, The (painting), 77
della Robbia, Giovanni, 64
Descent from the Cross (painting), 62
Design in America: The Cranbrook Vision 1925–1950 (exhibit), 102–3
Detroit, Michigan
   landmark structures, *162–63*
Detroit Arts Commission, 170
Detroit Club, *162–63, 166–67*
Detroit Evening News, 18, 164
Detroit Institute of Arts, 21, 102, *162–63, 170*–71
Detroit News, 8, 164
   Building, 26, *162–63, 165–66*
Detroit School of Design, 97
Detroit Society of Arts and Crafts, 1, 6, 18–19, 30, 32, 42, 62, 97, 102, 171
   history of (Colby), 10n
Detroit Trust Company, 41
Detroit Urban League, 19, *162–53, 168*
   See also under Albert and Ernestine Krolik Kahn House
Diana Courtyard, 130

Diana (sculpture), 130
Dining Hall, *68–69,* 86, *88–89*
Dinkeloo, John, 157
Diogenes (sculpture), 79
Discus Thrower, The (sculpture), *82*
Dodge, Alfred G., 23
Dodge, John, 23
dormitories, 71, *86–87,* 94, 105, 112, 127, 129, 132–*34*

Eade, Mary, 41
Eames, Charles, 103, 147, 156
Eastman, Winifred, 154
Eichstaedt, Edward A., 128, 137
Eliel and Louise Gesellius Saarinen House, 9, *94–95, 106–7,* 108–*9,* 110
Ellerhusen, Ulric, 60
Endicott, Mary Elizabeth Booth, 40
English Renaissance style, 19
    See also under Kahn, Albert
Episcopal Church, 54–55, 70, 126
Erb, Barbara, 146
Erb, Fred, 146
Erb Family Science Garden, 29, *138–39,* 145, 149–*50, 151*
    "House of Ice," 150–*51*
    "House of Vapor," 150
Eschmann, Jean, 100, 105
Europa and the Bull (sculpture), 96, 115, *119,* 121
Evans, David, 82
Evening News Association, 8, 18
Eyre, Wilson, Jr., 166

Faculty Row. *See* Faculty Way Houses
Faculty Way Houses, *68–69,* 91
Fenton, Michigan
    Community Center, *152–53, 161*
Festival of the May Queen (tapestry), 133
Filler, Martin, 96, 129
Fisher Building, 73
Flagstaff Hill, 20
Floegel, Alfred E., 64
Folke Filblyter on a Horse (sculpture), *117*
Fontana Della Tartarughe (sculpture), 28
Ford, Clara Bryant, 23
Ford, Edsel Bryant, 170
    home of, 23
Ford, Eleanor Clay, 23, 170
Ford, Henry
    Fair Lane home, 23
Ford Motor Company, 54–55
Fredericks, Marshall M., 31, *33,* 101, 135, 137
frescoes, 58, 62–63
Friedlander, Leo, 60
Friendship Arch. *See* Gateway of Friendship
Fuller, Buckminster, 156

Galileo Portal, *78–79*
Gallagher, Percival, 56, 66
Gallante, Ted, 12, 15
Gannett Company, Inc., 8
gardens, 2, 8, 16, 22, *28–29,* 32–33, 97, 99, 114–15, 138, *150–51*
Gate Lodge, *122–23,* 128
Gateway of Friendship, 75–76
    inscriptions, 87
Gateway to the Campus. *See* Woodward Avenue: entrance on
Gavin, Robert M., Jr., vii–ix, 9
Gehry, Frank O., 147
General Motors Corporation. *See* General Motors Technological Center

General Motors Technological Center, 152, *160*
George Washington, Portrait of, 88
Gesellius, Herman, 109
Gift of Knowledge, The (chimneypiece), 80
Gilbert, Cass, 170
glass, ornamental, *63*
glass, stained. *See* stained glass
Goldberger, Paul, 9–10n
Goodhue, Bertram G., and Associates, 5, 55–57, 59, 62, 64, 66
Goodhue, Harry Wright, 62
Gordon, James C. *See* James C. Gordon Hall of Science
Gothic Revival style, 5, 19, 23, 27, 55–56, 117, 169
Graves, Michael, 147
Great Crusade, The (tapestry), 27
Greek Theatre, 9, *16–17,* 21, 30–*31,* 32–*33,* 142
Greenwood Cemetery, *152–53, 158*
Gregory, Waylande DeSantis, 105
Grindley, Mary Alice, 31, 137
Grindley, Robert, 137
Grosse Pointe, Michigan, 73, 137
Grotel, Maija, 101, 160
Grylls, H. J. Maxwell, 171
gymnasiums, *38–39, 45,* 83, *122–23,* 129

Hall of Science. *See* James C. Gordon Hall of Science
Harley, Ellington, Cowin, and Stirton, 170
Headmaster's House, *94–95,* 104, 111–12
Headmistress's Residence (Robin Hill), *122–23,* 137
Hedgegate. *See* Hedgegate Apartments
Hedgegate Apartments, *16–17,* 23, *37,* 97
Hellmuth, Obata & Kassabaum, 8
Herbst, George, 8
Hermes (sculpture), *82*
Herter, Albert, 27
Hession, John, 80
Hewlett, Tom, 45
Hitchcock, Henry Russell, 129
Hlafter, Jon, 8
Hoey, Harry D, 77
Hoey Hall, 45, *68–69,* 71, *75,* 77, *78–80,* 81
    study/library wing, 80–81
Hoey Tower. *See* Hoey Hall
Hoffman, Dan, 8–9, 15, 45, 50, 150
    as architect-in-residence, 12–13
Hogan, James H., 60–*61,* 64
Holiday Tables, 22–23
Holl, Steven, viii, 140, 145–47
Honore, Paul, 172
Hopkin, Robert, 172
housing, faculty. *See* Faculty Way Houses; Valley Way Houses
housing, staff. *See* Valley Way Houses
Hudson, Joseph L.
    Claireview home, 32
Hulbert, Henry Schoolcraft, 6, 99
Hunter Boulevard. *See* Woodward Boulevard
Hymn to Brookside, 49

Infirmaries, *68–69, 90,* 134
Institute Way, 12. 143, 145
Intermediate Art School, 101
Irving and Casson, *63*
Italian Boathouse, *16–17, 35*
Italian Cottage, 97

James C. Gordon Hall of Science, *68–69,* 83, 90–*91*
Jenney, William LeBaron, 33

Jensen, Jens, 23, 33, 137
Jickling, Lyman and Powell, 114
Johnson, Johnson & Roy, 11, 30, 33
Jonah and the Whale (sculpture), *94–95*, 96, 111–12, *113*
Jungwirth, Joseph, 43, 168
Junior Dormitory. *See* Marquis Hall

Kahn, Albert, 1, 5, 19–20, 23–24, 26–27, 29–30, 33, 73, 97, 125, 137, 168, 171, 172
    See also Albert and Ernestine Kahn House
Kahn, Ernestine Krolik, 168
Kahn, Julius, 20, 168
Kahn, Louis, 156
Kahn, Moritz, 20
Kahn House. *See* Albert and Ernestine Kahn House
Kapp, William Edward, 23, 143–45
Kennel Apartments. *See* Carriage House
Keppel, Charles J., 83
Keppel Gymnasium, *68–69*, 83, 85, 90
Kerr, Peter, 76
Kessler, William, and Associates, 12, 171
Kevin Roche, John Dinkeloo, and Associates, 157
Kiley-Walker Designs, 170
Kingswood, Elizabeth, 126
Kingswood Lake, 1, 3, 21–22, 28, 35, 124, 129, 137, 141
Kingswood School, vii, 1, 5, 9, 13, 28, 100, 112, *122–23*, 128–30, *131–32*, *133–34*
    aerial views of, *7, 125*
    Dining Hall, *6*, 127, *132–33*
    entrance gates, *6*, 13, *122–23*, 127
    Green Lobby, *130–31*
    infirmary, 131
    merger with Cranbrook School, 73
    motto, 127
    oval turning circle, *122–23*, *128–29*
    Wenger Gymnasium, *135–36*, 137
    See also under Cranbrook Kingswood Upper School
Kirchmayer, John, 24, *26–27*, 42–43, 62, *64*, 169
Kirk, Arthur Nevill, 36, 62, 64, 105
Kivi's Muse (sculpture), 107
Kleckner, Keith, 8
Knoll, Florence, 103
Koralewski, Frank, 24, 64
Korbell, Mario, 24

Lahser Road, 106
Lake Jonah, 96
landscaping, viii, 1, 3, 5, 9, 13, 19, 33, 56, 66, 75, 96, 137, 145
Lang, Alois, 62
Lawrie, Lee, 60
Leipold, Albert, 62
Lerchen Hall, *68–69*, 81–*82*
libraries, *26*, 42, 44–*45*, 58, 71, *80*–81, 94, 96–97, 99, 102, 114–17, 129–31, 152
Light Pylon. *See* Cranbrook Institute of Science
Lindgren, Armas, 109
Lindquist, Rudolph, 111
Lindquist Hall. *See* James C. Gordon Hall of Science
Little Gym. *See* Lerchen Hall
Log Jam Arch, *38–39*, 45, *49*
Lone Pine Inn, 40, *152–54*, *155*
Lone Pine Road, 1–2, 9, 11, 19, *24*, 31, 40, 54, 56, 66, 74, 90, 96, 99, 103, 105–6, 142
Long Lake Road, 154
Lorch, Emil, 97–98

Lower Grotto Lake, 22
Ludowici Celadon Company, 77, 107

McEwen, Alexandrine, 171
McEwen, Katherine, 171
    dining hall paintings by, 88
    frescoes by, 42, 62–63
Machado, Rudolfo, 12
McMath, Robert R., 144
McMath Planetarium, *138–39, 143–44*
Macomb County, Michigan, 160
Macomber, Henry P., 100
Maija Grotell Court, *105*
    See also Grotell, Maija
Mailbox Pavilion, 13
Main Entrance Gate. *See* Peacock Gate
Manship, Paul, 24. *76*
Mantynen, Jussi, 121
Map of North America Depicting the Principal Expeditions of Discovery and Exploration, 80
Maps
    Bloomfield Hills, Birmingham, Warren, and Fenton, Walk Eight, *152–53*
    Brookside Lower School, Walk Two, *38–39*
    Christ Church Cranbrook, Walk Three, *52–53*
    Cranbrook Academy of Art, Walk Five, *94–95*
    Cranbrook Institute of Science, Walk Seven, *138–39*
    Cranbrook Kingswood Upper School, Walk Four, *68–69*
    Detroit Landmarks, Walk Nine, *162–63*
    Homestead Properties, Walk One, *16–17*
    Kingswood Campus, Walk Six, *122–23*
Maroti, Geza, 44–*45*, 72–73, *78*–80, 100, 103, 106
Marquis, Rev. Samuel Simpson, 6, 54–56, 64, 99, 169
Marquis Arch, *86*
Marquis Hall, *68–69*, 75, *86*–87
Mason and Rice, 19–20, 54, 164
master plans, 8–9
Master's Club, 87
Mayers, Murray and Phillip, 56, 59
McMath Planetarium, *138–39*
Meeting House, The, 5, *38–39*, 40–41, *42*–42–*43*, 44–*45*, 54, 63, 126
Meiere, Hildreth, 62
Mercer, Henry
Mermaids and Tritons (sculpture), *145*
Michigan Society of Architects
    award to Eero Saarinen, 156
Mill House, *16–17*, 35
Miller, Edward A., 105
Milles, Carl Emil Anderson, 91, 100, 106
    sculptures by, ix, *104*–5, 111–12, *113*–15, *117, 119*–21, 130, 137, 143, 145
Milles, Olga Granner, 110–11
Milles House. *See* Carl Emil Anderson and Olga Granner Milles House
Milles Studio, *94–95*, 111–12
Mitchell, Wallace, 101
Moneo, Jose Rafael, viii, 96, 117
    as recipient of Pritzker Architecture Prize, 118
Morris, May, 32
Morris, William, 1, 32, 35, 42, 55, 110
    See also Arts and Crafts style
Morris and Company (England), 63
Morris Mill, 22
    See also Mill House
mosaics, 58, 60, 62
Mother Goose figures, 43
Murray, Oscar H., 5, 55–56, 62, 64, 66

museums, 1–2, 94, 96–97, 99, 102
Music Building, 68–69, 90–91

National Historic Landmark designations, vii, 9, 23
Nettleton, George, 20
Nichols, Walter, 114, 127
Nichols Gate, 94–95, 96, 114–15
Nyrop, Martin, 72

Oakland County, Michigan, 40, 154, 158
    geology of, 1, 15, 25
Oakland University, 24
O'Dell, Hewlett and Luckenbach, 45, 135, 137
Old Mud Mill. See Mill House
Olmsted Brothers, 56, 66
Orchard Ridge Road, 111
Oriental Garden, 16–17, 34
Orpheus Fountain, 114–15, 120–21
Osler, Peter, 83, 119–20, 145, 150
Ostberg, Ragnar, 72
Our Brookside (mosaic), 48

Page, Rt. Rev. Herman, 55, 57, 87
Page Hall, 68–69, 75, 86–87, 88
pageants, 74
Pair of Running Boars, A (sculpture), 145
Pair of Running Deer, A (sculpture), 105
Pallasmaa, Juhani, 12, 15
Panama-Pacific Exposition (1915)
    influence on Oriental Garden (see), 34
Pankration (sculpture), 81
Parke-Lone Pine House. See Lone Pine Inn
Parker, Leonard S., 157
Paulsen, Glen, 157
Peace Memorial (sculpture), 111
Peacock Gate, 68–69, 74–76
Peale, Rembrandt, 88
Pelican and Chicks (sculpture), 44–45, 45
Pelli, Cesar, 157
Persephone, Goddess of Spring (statue), 31, 33
Pewabic Pottery, 9, 24, 36, 60, 77, 108, 130,
    162–63, 169, 173
Pickle Island, 38–39, 50
Platt, C. De Forrest, 75
Pohndorf Collection, 141
Pontiac, Michigan, 73
Pope, Gustavus D., 6, 99
Powell, James, 60
Prairie style, 5, 20, 23, 33, 128–29
Precepts Governing Cranbrook (Saarinen), 103,
    141–42

Quadrangle, Cranbrook School. See Cranbrook
    School Quadrangle
Quadrangle Fountain, 75, 140
Quinn/Evans Architects, 30, 33

Rackham, Horace H., 161
Rackham, Mary A., 161
Rainbow Fountain, 44
Ram House, 21–22, 44
Ramsden, Omar, 24
Reflecting Pool. See Cranbrook Institute of
    Science
Reflections Cafe, 144
Renwick, James, 55
reredos, 62, 64, 169
Richardsonian Romanesque style, 167, 170
River Rouge, 1, 23, 40, 46, 50, 91, 124, 140
    damming of, 3, 21, 44
Rivera, Diego, 171

Robert and Eva-Lisa (Pipsan) Saarinen Swanson
    House, 106, 152–53, 155
Robert E. Lee Group (sculpture), 91
Robin Hill. See Headmistress's Residence
Roche, Kevin, 157
Rock Garden. See Oriental Garden
Rose, Peter, viii, 9, 45–46
Ross, William F., and Company, 24, 27
Rudolph, Paul, 172

Saarinen, Aline B. Louchheim, 156
Saarinen, Eero, 76–77, 88, 90, 103, 107, 117, 130,
    133. 147, 156–57, 160–61
    See also under Vaughn-Saarinen House
Saarinen, Eero, and Associates
    Office, 152–53, 157
Saarinen, Eliel, vii–ix, 2, 4–6, 9, 13, 33, 49. 62,
    70–72, 73, 76, 79, 81–82, 86–88, 90–91,
    97–103, 105–12, 114–15, 117, 119, 125,
    127–30, 134, 140, 142–43, 145–47, 150–51,
    155, 157, 160–61
    furniture designed by, 108, 110
Saarinen, Louise (Loja) Gesellius, 72, 99–100,
    106–10, 130, 133, 155, 157
    studios of, 101, 105, 152, 156
Saarinen House. See Eliel and Louise Gesellius
    Saarinen House
Saarinen House and Garden: A Total Work of Art
    (Wittkopp), 107
Sacred Lion Dog (statue), 28, 96
Saginaw Road. See Woodward Avenue
Saginaw Trail. See Woodward Avenue
Saint Dunstan's Playhouse, 16–17, 33–34, 142
Saint Dunstan's Theater Guild, 34
Saint Paul's Cathedral, 162–63, 169
Scarab Club, 162–63, 172
sciences, 15, 140–42
    See also under Cranbrook Institute of Science
Scripps, Harriet Josephine Messenger, 18–19, 164
Scripps, James Edmund, 18–19, 164
Scripps house (Detroit), 19
Sculpture Department, 100
Sea of Galilee (lake), 56, 60
Senior Dormitory. See Stevens Hall
Sibley, Judge Solomon, 42
Silvetti, Jorge, 12
Simonds, Ossian Cole, 3, 30, 32
Siren with Fishes (sculpture), 104
Skillman, Robert H., 145
Skillman, Rose P., 145
Skillman Foundation, 145
Skillman Wing. See Cranbrook Institute of Science
Skogster, Greta, 108
Sloan, Rubin, 20–21
Smith, Hinchman and Grylls, 23
Smith, William, 43
Snyder, Robert H., 111
Snyder and Wilson Associates, 112
South Cranbrook, 56
stadium. See Thompson Oval and Stadium
stained glass, 43, 57–58, 60–61, 62, 79, 165
Stegosaurus (sculpture), 145
Steven Holl Architects, 146–47
Stevens, Henry G., 172
Stevens, William Oliver, 74, 87, 111
Stevens Hall, 68–69, 75, 86–87
Stevens Terrace, 87
Stiff's Flouring Mill. See Mill House
Stone, Arthur J., 24, 27
Stoney House, 21
"Story of Cranbrook, The" (essay), 98

Stratton, Mary Chase Perry, 1, 24, 36, 60, 108, 130, 169, 171, 173
Stratton, William Buck, 171–73
Strengell, Marianne, 101
studios, 94, *101*, 105, 110–12, 117–*18*, 129
Sukert, Lancelot, 172
Sullivan, Louis, 5, 10n
Sunken Garden, 28
Sunset Hill, 96, 99, 124–25, 140, 143
Sunset Terrace Houses. *See* Faculty Way Houses
Sven Hedin on a Camel (sculpture), 145
Swann, Lily, 156
Swanson, Eva Lisa (Pipsan) Saarinen, 70, 77, 100, 105–6, 130, 133, 155
Swanson, J. Robert F., 44, 70, 93, 97, 106, 155
Swanson, Robert Saarinen, 114, 117
Swanson, Ronald, 155
Swanson and Booth, 29, 37, 67, 70, 97, 103
Swanson House. *See* Robert and Eva-Lisa Saarinen Swanson House

Taft Group, 8
tapestries, 27, 57–58, *61, 108*
Tarapata/MacMahon/Paulsen (TMP), 75, 81, 90, 131
terraces, 5, *28,* 83, 87, 96, 115, 119, 133–34
Textile and Weaving Department, 100, 105
Thompson, Fred, 128
Thompson, Paul "Admiral," 82
Thompson Oval and Stadium, *68–69, 81–82*
Thornlea House, 5, *16–17,* 23, *36,* 47, 97
Thornlea Studio, 36
Touche Ross, 8
Tour Cottage. *See* Infirmary
Tower Cottage, *16–17,* 21, *29–30*
Tower Court, 76, 78
Towerknoll. *See* Robert and Eva-Lisa Saarinen Swanson House
Trellis Bridge, 13–*14*
Trinity Episcopal Church (Detroit), 19, *162–63, 164–65*
Triton Pool, 9, 96. 108, 115, *119–20*
Triton Pool Court, *94–95*
Triton (sculpture), *119–20*
Tsien, Billie, viii, 9, 83
Tudor style, 26, 30, 37, 93, 155, 159
Turnbach, Gladys, 126
Turtle Fountain, 28–*29*
Twin Cottage, *16–17,* 29–30
Two Girls Dancing (sculpture), *136*
Two Sisters (sculpture), *135,* 137

University of Michigan, 3, 5, 23, 33, 55, 70, 97–98, 103, 117

Valentiner, Dr. Wilheim, 170
Valley Farm Road Houses. *See* Valley Way Houses
Valley Way Houses, *68–69, 92*

Van Tine, William H., 23
Vaughan, Peter A., 93, 156
Vaughan Road, 11, 156
Vaughn-Saarinen House, 107, *152–53, 156*
Vaughn School, 1, 93
Venturi, Robert, 157
Vettraino, Michael (Mike), 3, 37, 62, 92
Viasic, Robert J., 50
Viasic Family Early Childhood Learning Center, 46, 48
Vienna secession style, 72, 98
    See also under Arts and Crafts style
Vinton Company, 20, 24
von Lossberg, Victor F., 62

Wallace, Grace Booth, 66
Wallace, Harold, 65
Walters, Parks, 29
Warren, Michigan, *152–53*
Waterworks Cascade, 21, 35
    See also under Mill house
Weese, Harry, 156
Wenger, Consuela S., 135
Wenger, Henry E., 135
Wenger Gymnasium, *122–23, 135–36,* 137
Wermuth, Albert, 106
Wermuth, Charles R., 56, 71
Wermuth and Son, 56–57, 106
West, Benjamin, 77
West Court. *See* Alumni Court
White, Lee A., 140
Williams, Tod, viii, 9, 83
Williams Natatorium, viii, 9. *68–69,* 75, *83–84,* 85, 96–97
continuity with outdoors in, 85
Wilson, Mathilda Dodge
    Meadow Brook Hall home, 23–24
Winter, Jessie T., 41, 45, 51
Wittkopp, Gregory, 107
Womanhood (stained glass), 60–*61*
Wonnberger, Annetta, 33
Wonnberger, Carl, 33
Wonnberger Court. *See* Greek Theatre
Woodland Wildflower Rescue Garden, 29, 151
Woodward Avenue, 8, 40, 71, 154, 158
    entrance on, *11–13, 14–15,* 142
Woodward Dream Cruise, 13
World War I, 27, 41, 154
World War II, 92, 102, 133, 158, 160
Wrestlers, The (sculpture), 81
Wright, Frank Lloyd, 129

Yamasaki, Leinweber and Associates, 172
Yellin, Samuel, *24–25*

Zantzinger, Borie and Medary, 170
Zonars, George, 114